Knowledge Management Strategy and Technology

For a listing of recent titles in the *Artech House Computing Library*, turn to the back of this book.

Knowledge Management Strategy and Technology

Richard F. Bellaver
John M. Lusa
Editors

Artech House
Boston • London
www.artechhouse.com

Library of Congress Cataloging-in-Publication Data
Knowledge management strategy and technology / Richard Bellaver, John Lusa, editors.
  p. cm. (Artech House computing library)
  Includes bibliographical references and index.
  ISBN 1-58053-105-9 (alk. paper)
    1. Knowledge management. 2. Information technology—management.
  3. Information networks—Management. 4. Internet—Management.
  I. Bellaver, Richard. II. Lusa, John M.

HD30.2 .K6377 2002
658.4'038--dc21   2001053530

British Library Cataloguing in Publication Data
  Knowledge management strategy and technology.—(Artech
  House computing library)
  1. Knowledge management 2. Knowledge management—Computer
  network resources
  I. Bellaver, Richard II. Lusa, John M.
  658.4'038

  ISBN 1580531059

Cover design by Gary Ragaglia

© 2002 Artech House
685 Canton Street
Norwood, MA 02062

10 9 8 7 6 5 4 3 2 1

Contents

7   An integrated development model for KM   113

8   The role of directories in KM   135

9   The Internet as a mechanism to enhance content and extend access to corporate data resources   151

10

A case study: the power of managing knowledge in a worldwide enterprise — 169

11

KM for competitive advantage: mining diverse sources for marketing intelligence — 181

Preface

This guidebook is meant to impress chief executive officers, chief financial officers, chief information officers, newly minted chief knowledge officers, and other key enterprise executives with the enormity and wealth of the information cache available to them from the lowest reaches of their enterprise to the farthest limits of the worldwide Internet. They will learn that knowledge management (KM) provides a focus to the enterprise when it acquires, stores, and utilizes knowledge-relevant information critical to tasks performed daily by organizational knowledge workers.

Chapter 1

A practical framework for understanding KM

Jay Edwin Gillette

The focus of this chapter is the central role of information in understanding data as a means of making decisions. Dr. Gillette defines information with the conclusion that information is composed of data to be understood as well as to make a decision or reinforce a position. To understand KM, it is necessary to understand relationships between essential types of knowledge and the critical "gateway" type of knowledge in the middle of them—information. This chapter provides a practical framework or model of these relationships, defining and relating knowledge as wisdom, understanding, information, data, facts, and phenomena.

Chapter 2

Document imaging and management: taming the paper tiger

Ronald J. Kovac and Donald S. Byers

The strategic goal of document imaging and management is simple—to reformat the paper form of unstructured data within an organization. This is done by effectively and efficiently inputting, storing, accessing, and using this information on the paper. The goal is met by taking all important paper documents and converting them into a structured electronic form. Once in this form the data within these documents can be stored, retrieved, managed, and otherwise used to make business decisions. The writers of this chapter explain that there are many benefits from taming the paper tiger of documents.

Chapter 3

Groupware: messaging and cooperation

Philip D. Campbell

In the broadest sense, groupware is any computer software product intended to enhance the ability of coworkers to work together. Many products fall under this definition that are not expressly marketed as groupware. E-mail systems, electronic bulletin boards, and the Internet itself, for example, are not often marketed as groupware, although all enhance group work. In this chapter, the writer takes a wide view of groupware. The focus is on the computer-mediated sharing of knowledge among members of groups and much less on whether or not the software being used is or is not officially groupware.

Chapter 4

Developing effective knowledge with both qualitative and quantitative research

Steve Jones and Elia Diamadatou

Using both quantitative and qualitative research methodologies to interact and help build an improved collection process will enhance the breadth and depth of data gathered, according to the writers. Focusing on just one methodology will limit the perspective of any research while using both methods provide more usable knowledge. Quantitative methods are considered more objective in their approach, providing greater accuracy in data delivered based on the level of variables controlled. On the other hand, qualitative methods are designed to examine all variables in the context with each other, rather than sorting out a single component and attempting to be unbiased while examining it.

Chapter 5

Systems architecture: the preparation for KM

Richard F. Bellaver

This chapter deals with the storage, identification, and quality of data, emphasizing the quality of those data, and explains the detail data planning, as well as the corporate planning, that must take place for an enterprise to derive any benefit from data mining. Besides attempting to optimize on new hardware and software, the phenomenon and the obsession with KM in American industry is having a profound effect on enterprise information technology planning. The practicality of distributed information systems and the desire to take advantage of the latest technology has led many to concentrate on cleaning up the databases and restructuring the processing.

Chapter 6

Data warehousing: the storage and access of distributed knowledge

Caitlin M. Groom and Frank M. Groom

In the past many efforts were made to create corporate decision support systems where staff information professionals attempted to collect a set of data that could be retrieved and brought to bear on a particular issue when a corporate officer needed to make an executive decision. Today the storage and access of these systems, sometimes called data warehousing, has become a crucial part of the learning and business process of many corporations. As H. G. Wells said in 1937, "Few people as yet, outside the world of expert librarians and museum curators and so forth, know how manageable well-ordered facts can be made, however multitudinous, and how swiftly and completely even the rarest visions and the most recondite matters can be recalled, once they have been put in place in a well-ordered scheme of reference and reproduction." There is no practical obstacle whatever now to the creation of an efficient index to all human knowledge, ideas, and achievements—to the creation, that is, of a complete planetary memory for all mankind. The technology is now available to fulfill Wells's prophecy.

Chapter 7

An integrated development model for KM

Feng Kwei Wang and Josh Plaskoff

The objective of the writers of this chapter is twofold. After defining some terms—namely, the commodity of interest (knowledge) and the process applied to it (KM)—they present an integrated development model for KM: one that addresses not only its technological aspects but also its organizational and process aspects. They go on to describe how this model plays out in the creation of a system at Eli Lilly and Company. Through this chapter, the executive reader gains a much more holistic perspective of KM and how to be able to prepare for design and implementation of KM initiatives.

Chapter 8

The role of directories in KM

Michael L. Simpson

Single-purpose, application-specific directories are scattered about every computer network, including the Internet, and most companies have quite a few. And since the information that is critical to employees doing their jobs is held and managed within the myriad business applications, the directory, in even its simplest form, becomes critical to accessing and managing everyday tasks of communication and business. The typical network user regularly spends 44 hours per year logging in to network applications. What's more, 70% of all help-desk calls are related to forgotten passwords. The writer addresses methods of dealing with creating efficiencies and gives specific examples of KM applications that are based on directories. He feels directories positively impact the efficiency in interaction of people to people, and even processes to processes.

Chapter 9

The Internet as a mechanism to enhance content and extend access to corporate data resources

Larry L. Learn

Enterprise data warehouses often fall far short of meeting the greater information needs of an organization in a timely manner. This is where the Internet can play a big role. It is this aspect of the role of the Internet in augmenting the systematic information resources of the enterprise—its total "data warehouse"—that will be the primary focus of this chapter. The Internet is an extremely valuable asset when it comes to data warehousing. Properly structured, the Internet provides a superb window on the data warehouse assembled by the enterprise, allowing extensive, economical, and timely access, using a nearly ubiquitous access platform—the Web.

Chapter 10

A case study: the power of managing knowledge in a worldwide enterprise

Ken Pratt

The success of the enterprise highlighted in this report depends, in part, on the effective exploitation of its technology base. With the solutions described in this chapter, the organization is demonstrating that knowledge sharing and using state-of-the-art information systems can make invaluable insights available at any time to its business operations anywhere in the world. Its approach to knowledge sharing is done with advanced content capture, management, and regeneration tools, such as text mining, knowledge landscaping, and cultural change. The platform allows knowledge workers, such as strategy analysts, to exploit a company's total knowledge resources as an assist in making their decisions more accurate and timely in business projects.

Chapter 11

KM for competitive advantage: mining diverse sources for marketing intelligence

B. J. Deering

The ideal data to use for understanding and managing competition varies with both enterprise objectives and the competitive situation being considered, according the writer of this chapter. Enterprise goals provide the focus both for specific competitor and customer attributes that are important, as well as for the level of data integrity needed to support the planning time frame. Creating new knowledge for competitive situations requires openness to an enlarged array of data sources and the ability to capitalize on developments in data modeling and mining, The prototype application of a modeling approach to KM described in this chapter clarifies how such openness can help manage competition.

Chapter 12

Building knowledge communities with webs of connections

Barbara Weaver Smith

A knowledge community is a web of connections among people with a common interest and a desire to learn. Knowledge communities connect people who know with people who want to know; collectively, the community knows more than each member knows individually. Members of a knowledge community do not merely exchange information; through dialog, they create new knowledge—knowledge that organizations are learning to leverage for innovation in products, processes, customer services, and trade.

Knowledge communities are natural human constructs. Each of us belongs to many knowledge communities—clubs, professional associations, faith institutions, and other social networks. But in the networked economy, corporations, such as *edmunds.com*, are deliberately employing new technology capabilities to create knowledge communities with their customers, suppliers, trading partners, and competitors.

Appendixes

A—Case Studies List
B—Bibliography
C—Glossary

Contributors

Introduction

K nowledge deficit is a metric that captures the costs and inefficiencies resulting primarily from intellectual rework, substandard performance, and inability to find knowledge information and expertise resources. According to the International Data Corporation, Fortune 500 companies were operating at a $12 billion knowledge deficit in 1999. This figure is expected to increase to $31.5 billion by 2003 as the percentage of knowledge workers in the work force increases from 20 percent in 1999 to over 40 percent in 2003.

This book is designed as a compendium of ideas to enlighten enterprise management to the methods and importance of transforming disparate information into knowledge in order to reduce some of that deficit. It is a guidebook that will impress upon chief executive officers, chief financial officers, chief information officers, newly minted chief knowledge officers, and other key enterprise executives the enormity and wealth of the information cache available to them from the lowest reaches of their enterprise to the farthest limits of the worldwide Internet. They will learn that knowledge can only be judged by its effectiveness and usefulness.

They will also learn that knowledge management (KM) provides a focus to the enterprise when it acquires, stores, and utilizes knowledge-relevant information critical to tasks performed daily by organizational knowledge workers. KM has a way of creating tremendous value by leveraging the intangible knowledge assets available to the enterprise and helping it gain insight and understanding from its own experiences as well. It must be made available freely throughout the enterprise. The concept of this sharing is not new. H. G. Wells, as early as 1937, predicted the "Permanent World Encyclopedia" and the concept of a world brain, but the technology wasn't ready to accomplish Wells's ideas. It is now. Jan Wyllie and the crew of the British-based *Trend Monitor* (www.trendmonitor.com) have been preparing managers and government officials about the opportunities and strategies of KM since 1995.

Readers of this book will discover that KM is essentially an art form and, subsequently, they will learn that the real art of management is managing knowledge. Knowledge is obtained in many ways, and executives wanting to save time and money must capitalize on the enterprise's intellectual property. In the final analysis, the readers of this book will learn that KM is the process of finding, selecting, organizing, distilling, and presenting information in a manner that strategically improves an enterprise's comprehension in many specific areas of interest, from marketing to employee training. Specific KM techniques assist the enterprise in such areas as problem solving, dynamic learning, strategic planning, and decision making. KM helps an enterprise gain insight and understanding from its own experience. Case histories are sprinkled throughout the book to illustrate this growing importance of KM.

There is a debate among some KM practitioners about the standard definition of "knowledge management." Some offer that KM does not even need a definition. Of course, some of us thought "virtual reality" would never stick either. The philosophy of this book will be that the overall definition is not very important. In fact, readers may see several definitions as they peruse the book. The mere words "knowledge management" may be just the latest buzzword to some. To others it has real meaning, maybe even a variety of meanings. That's what this book is all about.

While there seems to be a number of separate, if somewhat independent, KM elements, they are interrelated when viewed as knowledge, especially in the strategic sense. This disparate nature of KM is evident in the major headings of this book: work flow and document management, groupware, directories, qualitative measurements, enterprise storage systems, competitive intelligence, and others. Each chapter heading is certainly descriptive and meaningful. While this book concentrates on the parts, from various experts in the field, the reader will soon learn that the whole of KM is more than the sum of its parts.

The purpose of this book is twofold. First, lay a foundation of information theory in updated, meaningful terms. Then detail the techniques needed to identify, manage, flow control, store, and share access to information. The first six chapters lay the theoretical, philosophical, and practical foundation for the understanding of the pieces and parts that make up KM. Chapters 7 through 10 detail the practical functions of knowledge-based systems, from data mining through electronic commerce.

The final chapter provides the competitive and networking advantages of using techniques and specific methods for implementing KM systems. Included are case studies from enterprises employing KM techniques. The case studies show that in the opinion of users KM creates new levels of knowledge, providing value-added and competitive advantages. While the least-defined advantage of KM is cost justification, the case studies do indicate a definite level of actual savings, as well as other quantifiable advantages. In those instances where cost savings are not included, users provide a rationale for continuing with KM techniques. The classic measurement work for intangible assets, Professor P. K. McPherson's *Inclusive Value Measurement*, can be found at www.infoplex-uk.com. More measurement work by the consultant David Skyrme can also be found on the Web.

We have no particular recommendations for the organizational placement of the KM function. While some may choose to appoint a chief knowledge officer (CKO), others may not. What does come through is that the duties of the archivist, database administrator, IT executive, and others are now interrelated. In developing a modern KM system, it is important that turf battles not break out.

Top management needs to provide that top-down guidance to foster the speedy development of modern KM techniques. There needs to be a bottom-up buy-in to the strategic importance of acquiring, storing, and massaging information with modern KM techniques.

In these instances, where an enterprise feels compelled to appoint a CKO, it should be made clear that strategic knowledge will be made available conveniently, through electronic means, to those in the organization with a need for particular knowledge information. Since many in the enterprise need access to knowledge in some manner, it is difficult to rationalize an enterprise executive who acts as a "knowledge czar" with tight control and ownership of the system.

We want to be clear. We do not recommend tight control. We believe that knowledge-based information should be provided readily, freely, and in an enlightened manner to those who have an organizational function to use it for the betterment and strategic advantage of the enterprise.

Debra Amidon, another of the early leaders in identifying the KM phenomena (whose work can be found on the Web site www.entovation.com), has stated, "Interest in a new economic world order based upon intellectual capital has grown exponentially in both industrialized nations and developing countries around the world. Organizations are wrestling with the implications of such dynamic change in every aspect of our society. Enterprise leaders are laden with outdated management technologies, not suitable for such an unpredictable climate of opportunity. Indeed, the ability to effectively manage these bountiful, intangible resources may be the challenge of the twenty-first century." Are you prepared for the challenge?

Richard A. Bellaver
John M. Lusa
November 2001

CHAPTER

1

Contents

A practical framework for understanding KM

Jay Edwin Gillette

> Where is the wisdom we have lost in knowledge?
> Where is the knowledge we have lost in information?
> —*T. S. Eliot* [1]

1.1 Introduction

To understand knowledge management (KM), it is necessary to understand relationships between essential types of knowledge and critical "gateway" knowledge. This chapter provides a practical framework, or model, for these relationships: in effect, defining and relating knowledge as wisdom, understanding, information, data, facts, and phenomena. Information may be obtained from many sources. There is experiential, job, entertainment, and spiritually related information. In some cases we are bombarded by information. In other cases we must use all our senses to search for some specific idea.

1

The focus of this chapter is on the central role of information and understanding data in decision making. We'll define information as composed of "data that are understood, and used to make a decision or reinforce a position." The chapter will suggest ways to model information networking as "information content, information form or structure, information transmission or networking, and information technology."

Finally, an analysis is given of the actual practice of information networking in five stages: access, filtering, storage, retrieval, and using—in essence, providing a practical approach to understanding and organizing KM challenges and solutions as a means to help comprehend KM in our work or what we encounter as vendor solutions in the marketplace. This framework is used to better understand specific examples found in case studies and vendor offerings in the field of KM.

1.1.1   How we know what we know: understanding knowledge

The issue of KM is relatively new and compelling, yet the problem is old and established. The issue is knowledge about knowledge—how we know what we know. The branch of philosophy dedicated to the issue is epistemology, the theory of knowledge, sometimes defined as the science of knowledge.

Epistemology is an impressive word, coming into the English language in the middle of the nineteenth century, the time of the rise of broad-based science. Yet, the origin of the word epistemology is older and easier to use. It has practical meaning for people working in organizations today.

The theory of knowledge—epistemology—is based on the Greek word for knowledge, *episteme*, which comes from two simpler words meaning, to stand upon, or understanding, what we stand upon. In other words, knowledge is ultimately what we understand or what we use as a base. Knowledge is the foundation for our view of things, and knowledge is the basis of our actions: it is referred to accurately as our "knowledge base [2]."

Thus, KM comes down to what we understand. Then the practical issue becomes how we manage knowledge. How do we know what we know? How do we understand what we understand? This has been a business issue for centuries, but now it has migrated from the head office to the back office to the front line.

There are multiple definitions of KM. Because it's such a broad term covering a complex topic, KM has taken on many meanings. Bill Gates has written quite sensibly about it, as follows:

> As a general concept—to gather and organize information, disseminate the information to the people who need it, and constantly refine the information through analysis and collaboration—knowledge management is useful. But like reengineering before it, knowledge management has become infused with almost any meaning somebody want to associate with it. . . . So let's be clear on a couple of things first. Knowledge management as I use it here is not a software product or a software category. Knowledge management doesn't even start with technology. It starts with business objectives and processes and a recognition of the need to share information. Knowledge management is nothing more than managing information flow, getting the right information to the people who need it so that they can act on it quickly. [3]

Despite Gates's vested interest as a software provider in this critical declaration, he has made a real contribution to clarity—"let's be clear," he says—KM isn't about software or technology systems.

My view is that these are KM tools. Just as tools for carpentry are about carpentry and help us do carpentry work, the tools are not carpentry itself. So, too, do software and systems tools for KM help us manage knowledge, yet they are not KM themselves.

Note that Gates uses the keyword "information" six times to describe the essence of KM. In the end, he concludes "knowledge management is nothing more than managing information flow, getting the right information to the people who need it so that they can act on it quickly."

Other commentators have arrived at similar conclusions. Samples of definitions of KM are provided in Table 1.1.

Each of the commentators approaches the topic from a different angle. In the discussion that follows in the next section, each of the approaches can be fit into a comprehensive framework for understanding the key role of information in a scale of knowledge.

Information is how knowledge moves between things and people, and between people and people. That's why Gates emphasizes information flow. To make this key relationship easy to understand and remember, say "Information is knowledge in motion."

Table 1.1
Definitions and Characteristics of KM

Source	Definition and Characteristics
Thomas H. Davenport and Laurence Prusak. *Working Knowledge* (Boston: Harvard Business School Press, 1998). (Example of the most common definition of knowledge management, theoretical principles, and practical recommendations)	"Knowledge is a fluid mix of framed experience, values, contextual information, and expert insight that provides a framework for evaluating and incorporating new experiences and information. It originates and is applied in the minds of knowers. In organizations, it often becomes embedded not only in documents or repositories but also in organizational routines, processes, practices, and norms" (p. 5). Principles of knowledge management: ▶ Knowledge originates and resides in people's minds. ▶ Knowledge sharing requires trust. ▶ Technology enables new technology behaviors. ▶ Knowledge sharing must be encouraged and rewarded. ▶ Management support and resources are essential. ▶ Knowledge initiatives should begin with a pilot program. ▶ Quantitative and qualitative measurements are needed to evaluate the initiatives. ▶ Knowledge is creative and should be encouraged to develop in unexpected ways (p. 24).
Sources	**Definitions as Processes**
Spectrum Software, *Special Edition Microsoft Exchange Server 5.5* (New York: Macmillan Computer Publishing, 1997). Available on-line: http://www.itknowledge.com/reference/standard/0789715031/ch05/ch05.htm.	Knowledge management provides: ▶ Knowledge creation ▶ Knowledge retention ▶ Knowledge sharing ▶ Knowledge accounting ▶ Knowledge association ▶ Knowledge leveraging (p. 7).
J. Botkin, *Smart Business: How Knowledge Communities Can Revolutionize Your Company* (New York: The Free Press, 1999).	The process of capturing, sharing, and leveraging a company's collective expertise (p. 40).

Table 1.1 (continued)

Sources	Definitions as Processes
David A. Garvin, *Harvard Business Review on Knowledge Management* (Boston: Harvard Business School Press, 1998).	"A learning organization is an organization skilled at creating, acquiring, and transferring knowledge, and at modifying its behavior to reflect new knowledge and insights" (p. 51).
C. W. Holsapple and B. W. Andrew, *The Information Jungle* (Homewood, IL: Dow-Jones-Irwin Publishing, 1999)	Collecting, storing, organizing, maintaining, recalling, analyzing, creating, deriving, presenting, distributing, evaluating, applying various pieces of knowledge (p. 16).

1.2   Information is knowledge in motion

Information is a component of knowledge. It occupies a central position in a scale of knowledge from phenomena to wisdom. Information is the gateway of interpretation. Information is how we understand what to do. It's the basis of our understanding. But we don't know what information to look for and put together unless we understand it.

Information is one of the component parts of knowledge. There are many parts to knowledge. There are many kinds of knowledge. Here are some examples: knowledge from experiences, knowledge as skills, spiritual knowledge, and gender and cultural knowledge. And there are many names to call parts and kinds of knowledge. Yet for clarity, the six parts, or categories, of knowledge that I model are a place to begin: a point of departure.

In this approach, there are six component parts of knowledge. They are listed here, in order to take them into view at one glance:

1.   Wisdom;

2.   Understanding;

3.   Information;

4.   Data;

5.   Facts;

6.   Phenomena.

Next, one may ask, "What difference does it make if you start at the bottom, with phenomena? What if you start at the top, with wisdom? And can we start in the middle?" (see Table 1.2).

In actuality, the scale operates in both directions. In fact, wherever one begins on the scale, there are links—mental links or hyperlinks, as we say today—in both directions. Yet, because knowledge most often

Table 1.2
Information in a Scale of Knowledge

Information is a component of knowledge. It occupies a central position in a scale of knowledge from phenomena to wisdom. It is the signifier-signified interface; the gateway of interpretation.
Wisdom
The ability of discern, to make judgments. Discerning wisdom is based ultimately on difference or differences. Wisdom is the ability to discern difference. Wisdom guides understanding. Understanding informs wisdom.
Understanding
The ability to recognize, to comprehend, to surround, and to select information on the basis of wisdom. It means to know the implications of information. Understanding tells how to apply information, and what information to look for. Understanding means to know the significance of information signs. Understanding is the basis of research.
Information
Singular, and idea. A concept formed in the consciousness of the perceiver. Plural, a set of ideas or concepts. Specifically, and in its main function, information is data selected, filtered, and used to make a decision or to reinforce the user's position. Information is applied data. That is, the data are applied for useful purposes to the information user. Information is the useful data. Information value is intrinsically relative to the user.
Data
Organized facts. "Data" in Latin means "the givens." "Datum" is the singular, "a given." Data are processed, that is, structured, facts.
Facts
Representations of phenomena. A fact represents a phenomenon. Facts are signifiers of phenomena. Facts re-present phenomena.
Phenomena
Those which appear to be. Singular, "phenomenon," that which appears to be. Phenomena appear as knowledge in perception, as the are perceived. Properly, perceptions of phenomena are knowledge.

derives from perceptions of phenomena, a first exploration of knowledge should begin there. It should be placed on the bottom, as a foundation layer. In technology planning, we often call the foundation the "physical layer." That's a good way to think of phenomena. One could loosely translate this classical word as "things," or the "things that are," or "what we perceive to exist."

Then I suggest going up the scale through facts and data, noting the important place of information in the center. Finally, through understanding, we reach wisdom at the top. This is the route of knowledge based on experience—personal or organizational.

Yet, we may also begin at the top of the scale, with wisdom; however, we may have arrived at wisdom. We may start with wisdom that we know (a form of knowledge) and go down the scale, through understanding and information, to data, facts, and phenomena. Wisdom tells us what to look for in data, facts, and phenomena. It helps us to create information. This is often the route of formal education or cultural orientation, such as family or social upbringing. In organizations, this is generally the approach of formal training.

In the scale of knowledge, the most critical kind of knowledge is information. That is not to say it's the most important kind of knowledge. Yet, information has a critical function. It's a key point on the critical path of knowledge.

Information is the door that swings both ways. It's the doorway or gateway between—on one side—our perceptions of phenomena that we represent as facts and organize as data—and, on the other side, what we understand, guided by wisdom.

Information is where wisdom interacts with phenomena. Information is where phenomena reach wisdom.

Information is how knowledge moves from "out there" to "in here" and back, both for individuals and organizations. Information is knowledge on the move. Information is knowledge, moving.

The following is a brief analysis and discussion of the component parts of knowledge. Here is how to apply the analysis. By clarifying what kind of knowledge you are dealing with, you'll better understand how to manage it. From a practical perspective, for those working in organizational KM, develop some key questions. We know that to get the best answers we have to ask the right questions. Sample questions, such as the following help us understand what kinds of knowledge we have to manage:

- "What kinds of knowledge do we have?" Example: We have a lot of data.

- "What kinds of knowledge are the most important to our operation and success?" Example: We need information to understand what our customers think of our product.

- "What kinds of knowledge do we manage well?" Example: We are good at perceiving customer satisfaction through factual surveys.

- "What kinds of knowledge do we need to manage better?" Example: We need to understand what the important technical trends are, in the midst of conflicting data about technology shifts.

Here are the specific ways to define each of the component parts of knowledge. Obviously there is much more to say about each one. Toward clarity, these definitions and characterizations of the components of knowledge are points of departure.

1.2.1 Phenomena
Those that appear to be. Singular, "phenomenon," what appears to be. Phenomena appear as knowledge in perception, as they are perceived. Properly, perceptions of phenomena are a form of knowledge. Examples: What is it that we see in here in front of us or what are people buying?

1.2.2 Facts
Representations of phenomena. A fact represents a phenomenon. Facts are signifiers of phenomena. Facts represent phenomena (i.e., facts present phenomena again—literally, they "re-present" phenomena). Facts codify phenomena. Example phenomenon: There we perceive the phenomenon of a high mountain. Example facts: The mountain is in Colorado and called Pike's Peak. It is 14,110 feet in elevation. People are buying a particular kind of software.

1.2.3 Data
Organized facts. "Data" in Latin means "the givens." "Datum" is the singular, "a given." Data are processed—that is, structured—facts. Example

fact: Pike's Peak is over 14,000 feet high. Data: There are more than 50 peaks in Colorado over 14,000 feet high. Example data: People are buying a particular kind of software; sales are highest among professionals in the first quarter of the year. Revenue from the sales are a specific amount that we can track by month.

1.2.4 Information

Singular, an idea. A concept formed in the consciousness of the perceiver through understanding. Plural, a set of ideas or concepts. The word *idea* comes from the Greek word for "form." The Latin-based word *inform*, the root word for "information," means "a form in." Where in? In the consciousness of the perceiver. Then the idea is information.

Specifically, and in its main function, information is composed of data understood, selected, filtered, and used to make a decision or to reinforce the user's position.

Information is a set of applied data. That is, data are applied for useful purposes to the information user. Information is useful data. To define it informally: information is news you use. Information value is intrinsically relative to the user—that is, data in the stock market tables are useless to you if you have not invested in the market. But, if you have, then data in the stock tables can be turned into information for you, if you understand them.

Here's an easy way to check if data are information: do you understand the data? Can you "read" these data? Do you get these data? In American English we say "I get the idea!" "I get it" means "I understand it." The idea is the concept in the consciousness or in the mind. Sometimes we say "I see it in my mind's eye." That's another phrase for understanding "it" or conceiving it. And popularly today, there is the expression "I have no idea." In plain English: "I don't know."

Example of information: The software is tax software in the United States. We know for a fact that the government tax-filing deadline is April 15. We understand from these data that we can make money selling the tax software in the first quarter, but sales will likely drop after April 15.

1.2.5 Understanding

The ability to recognize, to comprehend, to surround, and to select information on the basis of wisdom. It means to know the implications of information. Understanding tells how to apply information, and what information to look for. Understanding means to know the significance of information signs. Understanding is the basis of research.

Understanding turns the abstraction of data into concrete information. Since we understand what these data mean, we can make a decision. Or we can reinforce our position, which is generally the result of decisions we've already made.

Understanding the information also points us in the direction of getting more data. It points us to where these data will be most useful. "Most useful" means turning the raw data into information that helps us make decisions, or reinforces our position.

This understanding may be the most important stage in practicing effective KM. Understanding data turns them into information we can act on. And, of course, understanding what we have before us—whether data, facts, or perceptions of the things that are—is what we mean in popular language when we say we are informed.

Example of understanding: I see that a certain stock's value has shifted, moving in response to announcements of government policy. I understand the stock's volatility is connected to the policy. I understand, based on historical data and competitive intelligence information that the government policy is presently stable. I will use that information to make a decision regarding whether to buy or sell the stock. That will require wisdom to come into play.

1.2.6 Wisdom

Wisdom is a topic that often dissolves into a kind of vague, floating infinity. Hypothetically, there may actually exist infinite wisdom or an infinite wisdom. Knowledge itself—as in the model of perceptions of phenomena, facts, data, information, understanding, and wisdom—may exist without end. There may be no boundaries to knowledge and, ultimately, wisdom. Wisdom is the ability to discern, to make judgments. Discerning wisdom is based ultimately on difference or differences. Wisdom is the ability to discern difference. In the scale of knowledge, wisdom and understanding are related. Wisdom guides understanding. Understanding informs wisdom.

Nowhere in professional life is knowledge more needed than knowledge as wisdom. Executives and leaders are really in the decision business. Leadership requires judgment most of all. Nearly every other form of knowledge can be managed more easily. It's wisdom that we need to manage best. Every leader eventually asks for wisdom.

With the scale of knowledge provided here, we see how wisdom receives information through the understanding of information. Wisdom takes into account what understanding provides, especially the significance of information. Wisdom then discerns differences. On the basis of differences—sometimes narrow, sometimes subtle, sometimes broad, sometimes obvious—wisdom makes a judgment between the differences.

Example of wisdom: From our understanding of the stock situation discussed previously, we discern the differences in the information. We know that the policy situation is stable, and thus we discern the stock price will remain stable. We judge whether or not to buy or sell on that basis. Our wisdom has processed our understanding and rendered a chosen path for our understanding to follow.

Managing to achieve wisdom is a great challenge. It often takes years. Yet, here's a paradox: Insights that we call wisdom may come to the inexperienced, or the youthful. That's why, in Tom Peters's approach to management, the wise leader will defer to the front line [4]. This paradox is even more significant in an organization, because wisdom relies on information networking from throughout the workforce.

1.3 Applying Gates's metaphor of a "digital nervous system"

This movement and use of information from across the organization is why Bill Gates has emphasized what might be considered a breakthrough insight he calls the "digital nervous system." The term hasn't taken off because of an unfortunate negative association of the word "nervous" in English. No manager wants to be considered nervous, though some of us may well be [5]. Yet the real nervous system in fact registers our perceptions and helps us take action. The body's nervous system is an information network and processor.

Gates thinks it's such an important concept that he incorporated it into the subtitle of his book, *Business @ the Speed of Thought: Using a Digital Nervous System*. He says it is in response to requests for more understanding of the concept of the digital nervous system that he wrote the book [6].

The power of Gates's metaphor and its relationship to KM is revealed through these words:

> To function in a digital age, we have developed a new digital infrastructure. It's like the human nervous system. The biological nervous system triggers your reflexes so that you can react quickly to danger or need. It gives you the information you need as you ponder issues and make choices. . . . A digital nervous system is the corporate, digital equivalent of the human nervous system, providing a well-integrated flow of information to the right part of the organization at the right time. . . . [I]t's distinguished from a mere network of computers by the accuracy, immediacy, and richness of the information it brings to knowledge workers and the insight and collaboration made possible by the information.

Through this discussion of information in a scale of knowledge with information in the privileged position of knowledge in motion, we have shown we can analyze knowledge into six related parts, or layers. In organizations, people lower in the organization's structure or knowledge base could handle the lower layers. Sometimes these processes can be automated.

Operating higher on the scale requires more knowledge and greater ability to make decisions. People operating at that level of knowledge are generally higher in the leadership dynamic of the organization. Yet it can be concluded that it is better to use the innate knowledge power of people throughout the organization to build our real knowledge base.

Every person uses some of these parts of knowledge all of the time, and all of the parts some of the time. The real challenge for organizations is to allow their people to use the entire scale of knowledge effectively. In the end, how well the whole organization performs information networking—how it moves and uses information—is the key to how well it will perform KM.

1.3.1 A four-layer model of the movement and use of information

So far information networking is defined as the movement and use of information. In a keyword analysis, we see that both words are keywords: information is networked, or networks move information.

Table 1.3
Information Networking Model

Content (Includes Information Management and Information Public Policy)	**Content:** What is contained in the information and its interaction with the other dimensions; information management and public policy of information included.
Form (Information Form and Information Structure)	**Form:** The applications of information; how the information is used by the end-client and how information form is affected by the other dimensions.
Transmission/Networking (Information Transmission and Information Networking)	**Transmission:** The methods used to move information from source to node to network; "Networking" proper.
Technology (Information Technology)	**Technology:** The physical basis in equipment and programming that allows the movement and use of information.

Information is a complex topic in itself. (In the full *Oxford English Dictionary,* the definitions centered on "inform" and "information" and associated terms go on for five pages.) A real challenge in organizational life is to define our organization's information. At the level we need here, we have defined information already in this discussion. Briefly, we said that information is composed of data we understand and use to make a decision or reinforce our position.

To clarify how information is moved and used in information networking is a practical matter. A four-layer model helps us understand the basic component parts (see Table 1.3). The four layers, representing the four component parts of information networking, are information content, information form or structure, information transmission or networking, and information technology.

All four layers are interrelated, and they affect each other. We separate the main functions of each layer for clarity, so that we know where we are in discussions. Many unclear discussions concerning information networking are caused by the fact that the participants are, in fact, talking about different layers but using similar language

Knowledge worker professionals need to understand all four layers and their interactions. Some may specialize in one or more layers but may need to comprehend and understand all four. Content specialists need to understand information technology, while networkers have to understand information form and structure and so on.

1.3.2 Relation of technology and transmission/networking

The bottom two layers are the technological foundation layers. These are the layers that engineering and technical professionals often specialize in. Conventionally, these were the concerns of technical education. Changes in these layers may make possible changes at the other layers.

Information technology of any kind fits in the foundation layer. A standalone computer can fit perfectly on that layer, even if it has no information content in it. Other examples of information technology are a pencil and paper, used together, or a film camera. Any information technology goes in that layer. Information technology is equipment, physical hardware, and software methods for information processing.

The next layer up is the actual movement of information—the methods used to move information from source to node to network to end user. This is "networking proper." The telephone and television industries call this layer "transmission," while computer and data processing industries call it "networking." In effect, they are the same layer—the layer where information moves. The relation between technology and transmission/networking is rich: changes in one layer rapidly can lead to changes in the other.

1.3.3 Relation of form and content

The top two layers are the classical component parts of information—information form and content. Conventionally, these were the concerns of education in the arts, and fields such as journalism, media, and writing. Changes in these areas, too, can affect the other layers.

The relationship between form and content is also rich. The key point is that the two elements interact. They influence each other. Content is to form as water is to a glass. The water needs the glass to be contained. The glass gives the water a shape. Information form shapes information content. That's why we talk about information structure, a term that means "form" in a way that is more clear to some. For our purposes, "structure" and "form" are equivalent.

Likewise, the glass doesn't make sense without water. Content fills form. Information content fills information form or structure. Content is the reason form exists. In the model, content also includes information management and information public policy. While there are concerns about technical standards, for example, almost all management and policy discussions ultimately return to content. Content is "what." Form and the other layers are usually "how." Information content almost always answers the ultimate management question, "What are we going to do, and why?"

In the world of KM, we need to keep the dynamic relationship of form and content in mind. We are in trouble if content has no form to give it shape. It's essentially knowledge with no place to go. That's the most common issue. We may know something, but how do we give it form? How do we structure it? How do we have an idea, a form, a conception—to conceive of the content? It's the source of the well-known, and truthful, reaction we hear when people say, "I have no idea."

Because the knowledge content in an organizational sense is often without structure, we arrive at the dilemma expressed in the title of O'Dell and Grayson's KM book, *If Only We Knew What We Know* [7].

Yet, we're also in trouble if we have form without content, such as memos without purpose, meetings without meaning. We turn in annual "objectives" lists that are too plain and too politicized to truly aim for in real action. This is an example of form without content. We might claim the content is actually the set of objectives, but they are empty objectives. Everyone knows it's just a matter form, "a formality." It's a matter of turning in a form, essentially. It's just going through the motions. In the complex, chaotic, dynamic times we are working in, when in doubt, sacrifice form for real content. It's true the concepts rely on each other, so we can't have one without the other. But content is king.

In information networking—the movement and use of information—all four layers come into play. Depending on what is being addressed, discussions of information networking can be separated into discussions about one layer or another. This is the fundamental concept of layered models: the separation of concerns. Putting things in layers helps us clarify complex relationships.

The way to use the four-layer model in discussion is to focus on which layer the people are talking about. Is it an information technology problem, or an information management problem? Are we concerned about how information or data are processed by a user—information technology, or how it gets to a user—information transmission or networking? The model helps us sort out the main part of the question. It helps us get to the point. The model helps us reach conclusions.

1.4   Moving and using information: the practice of information networking in a KM context

"Practice," in plain English, simply means "doing." The practice of information networking means how we move and use information. In a sense, the practice of information networking is what allows us to manage knowledge. Information networking is the backbone of KM.

Since knowledge is information on the move, how we "do" information—our practice of information networking—is how we are able to know what we know.

Again, with the goal of bringing clarity, the practice of information networking has five main parts (see Table 1.4). This is a significant contribution for organizations from the approach to KM. The main categories are information access, filtering, storage, retrieval, and using.

In general, information is moved and used through these five steps, most often in this order. From one person getting a document off his or her desk, to a multinational corporation sending an e-mail message, the process is similar. Even as you read these words, you are essentially going through these five steps in the movement of the words from the page through your short-term memory to your long-term memory and back to your active awareness that you use to understand the sentences.

Once again, to take in the entire analysis in one glance, the information is given in familiar written form. Here are the five main categories, followed by the second level of analysis of the main categories:

1.   Access (input, processing, movement, output)

2.   Filtering (display, selection, classification, prioritization)

3.   Storage (organization, placement, securing, indexing)

4.   Retrieval (searching, finding, bringing forth, queuing)

5.   Using (applying, deploying, presenting, distributing)

Reading this list, from top to bottom and left to right, shows the overall movement and use of information. The last category of using

Table 1.4
The Practice of Information Networking

Main Category of Information Networking	Second-Level Analysis of Information Networking Categories			
Access	Input	Processing	Movement	Output
Filtering	Display	Selection	Classification	Prioritization
Storage	Organization	Placement	Securing	Indexing
Retrieval	Searching	Finding	Bringing Forth	Queuing
Using	Applying	Deploying	Distributing	Presenting

information, distributing, then leads back into access, if the process is continuous.

There are a number of traditional computing and information management terms in these categories to show how traditional approaches fit into this overall analysis. Most of what we call "information management" can be located in these categories, and that is a useful feature of the analysis.

Certain categories could fit into more than one place—for example, "securing." This is a second-level category in information storage. We secure information after we have stored it through organization and placement. For example, in the physical world, in a workshop, you put your tools in a drawer of the toolbox, and then lock the toolbox.

Yet, security can also apply at the information access category. We might encrypt a message as we input it for security. In my analysis, that could become a deeper category, say at the third level of analysis, "input." And so on.

The purpose of this analysis of the practice of information networking is to help us understand where our own information practices fit in. The table gives an overall view for clarity, for a common language in discussing what we're actually doing as we move and use information, and as a guide to planning information networking initiatives.

From our perspective as people in the information economy, we are gaining more and more knowledge and expertise in the first steps of the practice of information networking. We have learned to access information well, through a long history of development in telephony, computer networking, and satellite transmission.

We are getting better and better at filtering information. Internet search programs, for instance, help us display and select, classify and prioritize information. The retrieval step and the storage step are spelled out in later chapters of this book. There has been much mechanical progress in these areas. There is still a great need to tap the knowledge holders to get the information we need and to put it into usable formats.

Finally, as people in the information economy, we have much more work to do in actually using information well, after we have successfully gone through the access, filtering, storage, and retrieval of information.

Yet even with much work to do in using information well, we are learning more and more about how to apply information. We are getting better at presenting it. Distributing it is a continuing challenge, if we mean effectively distributing it, so the right people have it at the right time, and not the wrong people, or at the wrong time. And deploying information, arguably the most strategic use of information and where executives and officers need to focus, is an area where we have the greatest challenges.

The real work of KM needs to move forward in these second-level categories of actually using information. These are the areas of the greatest effectiveness and the greatest payoff. In the information economy, using information effectively is the end goal of the massive explosion of activity in information access, filtering, storage, and retrieval.

1.5   Conclusion

Understanding the importance of KM leads to fundamental practical questions. If this is so important, why doesn't everybody do it, or do it well? As indicated, the real reason is that KM is complex. It is difficult to do it well. Yet the very barriers to entry that make it difficult also represent competitive advantages to those who can overcome the barriers. Not everyone can manage such a complex and profound undertaking. Yet the payoff beckons. Those who can, will do. These doers will be the winners.

1.5.1   The future of KM: distinctive trend or ubiquity

What will be the future of KM? One of the best answers to that question is by Ruggles and Holtshouse [8]. They believe the outcome of the KM movement will emerge as one of two main scenarios: distinctive trend or ubiquity. That is, KM will have a future either continuing as a distinct trend or becoming a ubiquitous part of all business practices.

In the distinctive trend scenario, KM will have a big impact, and then essentially become another management fad and fall out of favor. The Gartner Group boldly predicts this will happen by 2003, and then be rediscovered and come to full flower by 2010. Some organizations will perform KM, while others will not.

Regarding the ubiquity scenario, Ruggles and Holtshouse suggest the following:

> [I]t is quite possible that "knowledge management" will fade away as a standalone trend or organizational function, but that its practices, tools, and techniques will live on within organizations, incorporated into what are considered everyday good business practices. Because knowledge management may become more like a discipline than a project, we believe that its life cycle would copy that of quality rather than, say, business process reengineering. In this way, although the "quality movement" has left the center of many management discussions, quality itself hasn't. In fact, it became part of everything, in a way more powerful than if it were just one person's job.

We believe the ubiquity scenario is the one that will actually emerge. That scenario in fact itself grows out of—and subsumes—the distinctive trend KM represents today. If the ubiquity scenario emerges, then just as quality is everybody's business, so, too, will KM become everybody's business.

1.5.2 Future of technology: mechanized techniques

Regarding mechanized techniques to assist in KM there appear to be some product improvements on the horizon related to the five categories mentioned previously. Possibly, the more interesting developments to watch are the suites of technology and methodology specifically developed to handle multiple aspects of KM. Among the best known of these is Raven [9]. It will be marketed as a package rather than as a set of individual components and will have three major related components: expertise profiling/locating, a collaborative portal, and content tracking and analysis. Raven is a product of IBM's Lotus Corp. and is the compilation of several years of research from a plan formulated in 1999.

For instance, Raven's locator is a Web crawler that will seek out expertise. It will look at authored documents about selected subjects. Before expertise is attached, the users themselves can determine or edit their profile. In addition, Raven's content catalog component will create and maintain content maps that identify topics and analyze subject content by evaluating frequency, proximity to other topics, relationship to people, and a host of other measures. The catalog is constantly refreshed and maintained based on new content and usage data.

1.5.3   Recommendations

The following recommendations will help you understand KM:

- Work to understand and become familiar with knowledge complexity. Use a thrive-on-chaos approach. Use adaptive, self-organizing initiatives for handling knowledge, at every level of the scale of knowledge.

- Weed the garden of ideas, the basis of information: don't select at seedling level. Instead, weed and thin the ideas when they grow to clarity. Let understanding consult wisdom, before making decisions about what data to select and use or to reject and disregard.

- Anticipate normal human ego response to pulled ideas. Nurture and harvest the ideas that are going to flourish. Yet allow for a regeneration of seedling ideas. Nature generates far more seeds than are going to grow to maturity. Nature plays the odds in its favor. Consider yourself and the organization as a garden of information. Do you have a knowledge nursery? Do you have good information gardeners?

- Use the power of people to understand data processed from phenomena as information.

- Focus on information networking as the key to KM. From the phenomena on up, analyze your information in a scale of knowledge. Then build KM based on the levels of the information networking model and the categories in your own practice of information networking.

- Actively pursue wisdom to guide understanding. Work as hard and smart on gaining wisdom and understanding as on gaining facts and data. Encourage leadership at all levels to seek and display wisdom—the ability to discern and make judgments.

1.5.4   Overarching conclusion: humans know best—homo sapiens comes into its own

Finally, here is an overarching conclusion: the human species is making historical advances in KM. Therefore, we make an overarching recommendation: let humans do what humans do best—work with knowledge.

The industrial economy puts humans to work with things—making things through process work. We are the creatures that are adept at knowledge. Humans know best. Of all the remarkable things humans can do, we do knowledge best. This is the era of the knowledge worker. The era of process work is eclipsed. Today we are in an information economy, serving as the driver for a knowledge society. Thus, my prime recommendation is to put us foremost in the work of knowledge—to work on knowing, not on processing, or even making.

Endnotes

[1]   T. S. Eliot, *The Rock* (New York: Harcourt, Brace and Company, 1934), 7. My use of this Eliot quote for an epigraph is inspired by Robert Lucky, who used it to discuss information as a concept in his seminal book, *Silicon Dreams* (New York: St. Martin's Press, 1989), 20.

[2]   Etymology sources: *The Compact Edition of the Oxford English Dictionary* (Oxford: Oxford University Press, 1971), 884. The word entered the English language in 1856, according to this source. William Morris, ed., *American Heritage Dictionary of the English Language* (Boston: Houghton Mifflin, 1979), 441.

[3]   Bill Gates with Collins Hemingway, *Business @ the Speed of Thought: Using a Digital Nervous System* (New York: Warner Books, 1999), 238.

[4]   Tom Peters has outlined his view of deferring to the front line as a leadership component in *Thriving on Chaos: A Handbook for Management Revolution* (New York: Harper & Row, 1987).

[5]   Compare the title of Intel CEO Andrew S. Grove's book, *Only the Paranoid Survive: How to Exploit the Crisis Points that Challenge Every Company and Career* (New York: Doubleday, 1996).

[6]   Bill Gates on why he wrote the book: "[A] lot of the CEOs asked me for
       more information on the digital nervous system. As I've continued to flesh
       out my ideas and to speak on the topic, many other CEOs, business manag-
       ers, and information technology professionals have approached me for
       details. . . . This book is my response to those requests." (See [3].)

[7]   Carla O'Dell and C. Jackson Grayson, *If Only We Knew What We Know: The
       Transfer of Internal Knowledge and Best Practice* (New York: Free Press, 1998).

[8]   Rudy Ruggles and Dan Holtshouse, *The Knowledge Advantage: 14 Visionaries
       Define Marketplace Success in the New Economy* (Dover, NH: Capstone, 1999).

[9]   "First Raven Product Announced," KMWorld On-line, September 27, 2000.

Acknowledgments

I am grateful for the help in the development, research, preparation, and encouragement of this work by Dr. B. J. Deering of US West; Rebecca Perez of Eli Lilly
and Company; Martin Noufer of Intel; and master's candidates Rosalyn Adams-
Smith, Molly Erman, and Matt Martin (CICS); Jim Needham of Ball State University; and other colleagues. I am especially appreciative of the support and professionalism of Amy Clevenger, the administrative secretary of the Applied
Research Institute at the Center for Information and Communication Sciences.

                                                              Jay Edwin Gillette
                                                              November 2001

CHAPTER

2

Contents

Document imaging and management: taming the paper tiger

Ronald J. Kovac
Donald S. Byers

> It's not what you know,
> it's what you do with it that counts.
> —*Anonymous*

2.1 Introduction

We have all seen it happen. Situations where the right information was not in the right place at the right time. In our personal lives it causes us to miss our child's soccer game, miss stock market action, or fail to get a bargain. In our professional lives it causes companies to take the wrong direction, develop the wrong product, or fail to see societal needs. But how do we find the right information and then provide it at the right time to the right people? That is the ultimate goal of KM and a goal that unless met will discount all our efforts to generate and move information around—a goal that must be met to get success in our personal and professional lives.

Although information has always been an important aspect of our lives, and our world, its importance has grown acute in our current information age. Whole corporations, and maybe our whole societal fabric, are now based on knowledge and information. Unlike 100 years ago where physical capital was prime, today's world revolves around providing the information at the right time to the right people.

The field of KM attempts to seek out, manage, and provide the information necessary to make correct decisions for people and organizations. KM is initiated by first assessing, collecting, and managing the different types of information existent within organizations. Information exists essentially in three states within organizations: in thoughts and ideas, in structured data, and in unstructured data.

Thoughts and ideas of people are very fluid and transient and exist around the water cooler, in the lunchroom, and may never even emerge into words but stay as thoughts in people's minds.

Structured data exist on computers and are in the form of databases and spreadsheets.

Unstructured data are information in the forms of letters, memos, magazines, newspapers, e-mail, and flyers that exists usually on paper and manages to overtake one's desk and file cabinets. Unstructured data can be further broken down into electronic data (e-mails, spreadsheets, etc.) and paper data (memos, magazines, etc.).

This chapter will focus on this last element of information, unstructured paper data, and will bring forth the tools and strategies to provide a KM solution. Within document imaging and management (DIM) systems we will explore how to wrestle the "paper tiger" into a KM solution and therefore assist people and companies.

2.2   Information revolution

Maybe we can contest who coined the term "information revolution." Was it Daniel Bell or Alvin Toffler? What we cannot contest is that we are in the information revolution. Society, wealth, and companies are based on the commodity of information rather than manufacturing or agriculture. While these two previous phases of our world history are still necessary for survival, and while these two phases still generate large sums of money and work, it is obvious that the attention of the world and especially America is on the information revolution.

A few historical underpinnings of the field may help clarify the current situation. In the 1970s, large-scale, centralized data computing sites were popping up everywhere. Aimed at centralizing and making more efficient the process of information calculation and transfer, these sites changed the world. Closer to home, in the office environment we found typewriters, copy machines, and dictation devices as more down-to-earth technologies that made our life easier.

The ability to create information was growing, and the media of paper and microfilm were the large-scale repositories of this newly created information. The 1980s brought the advent of personalized computing and with it the ability to generate information at astounding rates. Add to this the fax machine and you can see a spiraling ability to create and move information.

The 1990s added to the mix, creating the networks to connect all these devices together. Fax machine, personal computer, mainframe computer, word processors, and the like could all be on the same "net" and therefore information could be generated and disseminated easily (see Figure 2.1).

But the aforementioned products and rate of information escalation were focused on the structured data of the organization and were mainly concerned with the generation and movement of these data. Information was easily created, massaged, shipped, and managed. But these efforts were toward structured information and not the unstructured paper

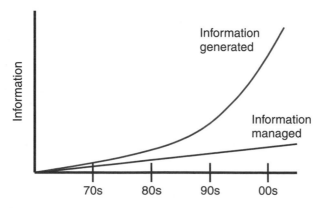

Figure 2.1   Growth of electronic information.

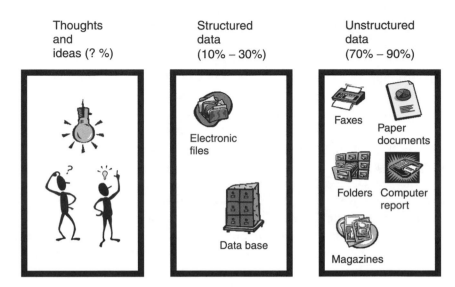

Figure 2.2   Percentage of information in corporate environments.

information. Although much has been heard since the 1970s about the paperless office, we all recognize by now that it will only come with the paperless bathroom.

Structured data exist in electronic ways. Computer-generated and maintained data are structured, and much energy goes into keeping this information readily available and easy to access. The whole revolution of the Internet is to provide more immediate access to the structured data of our world. The ability to log into a computer in Washington and see your Social Security account is both fascinating and useful. The structured world continues to amaze.

But unstructured data, consisting primarily of paper documents (computer reports, faxes, and other nonelectronic forms of communications) comprise 70% to 80% of the information within corporate America! (See Figure 2.2.) It seems odd that so much time and energy is spent making structured data easily accessible and usable when only 10% to 30% of the information is maintained in this form. KM, to be truly all encompassing, must cover both the structured and unstructured arena.

2.2.1   The business case

What is becoming apparent is that information generation and dissemination is growing far quicker than the ability to manage and access this information. This is especially true in the unstructured information world where information management systems are generally lacking. This flies in the face of the challenges of today's business world, which include the following:

> Increasing business volume without increasing headcount;

> Improving customer service;

> Reducing time to market for products;

> Minimizing exposure to legal or regulatory actions.

Consider some data that have been recently introduced. According to the Gartner Group [1], knowledge workers spend 20% of their work time performing document management in nonautomated environments. Call this paper shuffling or whatever, highly paid programmers, engineers, technicians, designers, and management are sorting through volumes of paper documents, binders, technical drawing cabinets, and invoices to find the important fact that will resolve the issue at hand. Does this meet the business challenges stated previously?

A recent Nielson report notes that it costs $20 to file and retrieve a document, but, if it is misfiled, it costs $120 to properly retrieve it. Given the volume of paper in an office, one could conjecture that probably 10% of the documents filed are done so improperly.

Added to this is the fact that American business generates about 90 billion documents per year, and each of these documents is copied an average of 11 times. Each of these copies is filed and possibly retrieved. The costs in manpower, paper, file cabinets, and space are enormous.

A final fact is that a typical organization of 1,000 people wastes over $11 million per year through manual document handling and management (Gartner Group). These costs come directly from company profits.

All these aforementioned facts point to an abundant amount of money being spent to "deal" with the paper tiger of the organization. These funds come out of the profit side of an organization. Let's consider that it usually takes $13 of gross revenue to make $1 profit. In order to generate more profit we can either get $13 more in revenue, or we can save $1 on the overhead side. A distinct benefit of DIM is that besides managing and providing information, it also reduces overhead costs tremendously within an organization, thereby increasing profitability.

It has been overheard that in a typical aircraft carrier, two feet of the water draft is generated due to the paper documentation carried onboard for the various systems.

2.2.2 What is document imaging and management?
The strategic goal of DIM is simple—to reformat the paper form of unstructured data within an organization. This is done by effectively and efficiently inputting, storing, accessing, and using this information on the paper. The goal is met by taking all important paper documents and converting them into a structured electronic form. Once in this form the data within these documents can be stored, retrieved, managed, and otherwise used to make business decisions.

But, how do companies benefit from this? There are many benefits from taming the paper tiger (besides a clearer desk), and a few follow:

1. *Managing the information in a common repository.* Rather than trace down the filed copy of the information or reviewing all paper copies looking for references to a topic, DIM offers a common researchable database.

2. *Ensuring proper handling and release of documents.* Documents once brought into a DIM system can be better controlled and used through a common repository.

3. *Meeting regulatory requirements.* Rather than maintaining the voluminous paper records for federal and state regulatory requirements, the pertinent data can now be stored and accessed electronically.

4. *Reducing liability by ensuring the use of the correct document.* With the wrong information disseminated companies are liable. In electronic form, the information is subject to faster revision and better control of these revisions.

5. *Reducing cost.* As noted before, managing paper in its true form is manpower intensive, slow, space intensive, and expensive. It has been noted that DIM systems usually recover payback for the cost for implementation within a year.

2.3 System solutions

Before we delve into what is necessary for a DIM system to operate, we will look at how DIM has assisted a particular company in taming the paper tiger. The case study is representative of the many that have embraced DIM and highlights the its stages and benefits.

2.3.1 American Electric Power

American Electric Power (AEP) [2] is a leading supplier of electricity and energy-related services throughout the world. In the United States, AEP provides electricity to parts of Ohio, Michigan, Indiana, Kentucky, West Virginia, Virginia, and Tennessee and operates a 1,900-mile natural gas pipeline and related facilities in Louisiana.

In December 1997, AEP agreed to merge with Central and South West Corp., a public utility holding company based in Dallas, Texas, that has operations in Texas, Oklahoma, Arkansas, and Louisiana.

AEP has consolidated its accounts payable activities across all of its regional power companies into a single processing location. Crowe, Chizek and Company LLP [3] (a Big 10 consulting firm) had implemented a document imaging and workflow system in the accounts payable department to accommodate this consolidation. The project was initiated in August 1995, and the original pilot implementation was completed in July 1996 for one of AEP's regional utility companies. The consolidated environment was implemented in September 1997, with full production for all AEP companies to be completed by mid-1998.

The system is client-server based with Windows NT 3.51 and Windows 95 clients and an IBM RS/6000 UNIX server. The core imaging system is FileNET's WorkFlo Business Systems product used in conjunction with FileNET's WorkFlo/Payables application.

AEP needed to consolidate and improve its 32-year-old accounts payable application, and the company asked Crowe, Chizek to help. Together, they identified the need for a flexible application to meet changing requirements with easier and more timely access to information using leading-edge technology. The customer also needed to increase productivity and reduce costs, while solving a Y2K compliance issue of its legacy accounts payable system. The most significant challenge centered upon the consolidation of six decentralized A/P locations with over 100 A/P employees into a single centralized location with less

than 50 employees while improving the timeliness of payments and providing easier and more complete access to payable information.

Crowe, Chizek assisted AEP with an accounts payable application
that electronically captures an image of incoming invoices, manages and
controls the routing and approval process, and allows entry of the
approved invoice into the system. Related approval documents may be
scanned and displayed to users during invoice processing to assist in
approving an invoice for payment. The application reduced man-hours
required to process invoices and eliminated paper-based purchase order
history files and paper document jackets.

The A/P application has allowed the customer to increase productivity from 7,000 invoices per clerk to 15,000 invoices per clerk while
decreasing the processing cost per invoice from $2.50 to $1.25. Electronic
routing and approval of invoices now permits same day routing and
invoice approval, with expanded work tracking and throughput statistics.

AEP has also implemented PeopleSoft [4] Accounts Payable for all
corporate accounts payable operations. Vendor invoices are scanned into
the workflow environment, segregated into PO and non-PO invoices,
assigned to an AEP business unit, and routed to a work queue for processing. Clerks in the accounts payable department are granted access to
these work queues based upon the business units with which each clerk
works.

The PeopleSoft invoice entry process has been altered to prompt the
user for the business unit to process a PO or non-PO indicator. The next
available new invoice is retrieved from the selected business unit's PO or
non-PO work queue and displayed to the user, along with the PeopleSoft
invoice entry form. The user may complete the data entry of the invoice
into PeopleSoft or route the invoice to a supervisor work queue for error
resolution and potential reroute to a different business unit work queue.

If the invoice is entered into PeopleSoft, index data on the invoice
image is updated with selected invoice data fields from the PeopleSoft
application to identify the invoice image within the imaging system and
link it to the PeopleSoft voucher. The invoice is then removed from the
work queue and the user continues with the next available invoice in the
queue.

2.3.2 The railroad system

The Railroad Retirement Board (RRB) [5] administers retirement-survivor and unemployment-sickness benefits for the nation's railroad work-

ers and their families under the Railroad Retirement and Railroad Unemployment Insurance Acts. In 1998, the RRB provided approximately $8.2 billion in benefits to over 772,000 beneficiaries. The RRB creates approximately 12,000 new paper-based claim folders each year, and 150,000 claim folders are accessed for adjustment or inquiry.

The benefit program is nearing completion of its migration from this paper claim folder system. The RRB file bank consists of over 1.3 million folders maintained in an off-site storage facility managed under contract with the National Archives and Records Administration's (NARA) Federal Records Center.

"With the paper-based folder system, we have to pay a fee for each folder retrieved, each folder refiled, a messenger service fee for the 100 million documents stored at the facility, as well as square footage charges," said Ken Zoll, chief of systems development at the RRB. "It has become exceedingly expensive and time consuming."

While the RRB did have an imaging system in place, an upgrade was sought that could interface with the Social Security Administration's imaging and workflow system, due to the significant benefit information and processing exchanges between the two agencies. However, the legacy system contained over 1 million images.

"Eastman Software/Vredenburg provided a cost-effective solution to meet our document imaging and workflow requirements," said Zoll. In September 1999, with the sickness benefits replacement system up and running, the RRB shifted its focus to the retirement folder process and purchased an additional 150-seat user license to begin the imaging of the retirement survivor documents. In addition, additional scanners, servers, and jukeboxes were purchased and installed for this expanded system.

The RRB issues retirement-survivor checks to close to 900,000 individuals every month and maintains records for 250,000 active employees. "The biggest savings we will see by implementing the document imaging and workflow system will be in storage and retrieval fees as well as in reduced labor costs," said Zoll. "Within three years the benefits-costs analysis projected is that annual savings will exceed $1 million."

2.3.3 The bank solution

Managing the operations of a large national bank comes with unique problems. For Banco Hipotecarios S.A. [6], some of its problems have been solved with document imaging and database technology. Banco Hipotecarios is Argentina's largest mortgage bank with $4.67 billion in assets, a 41.6 market share, and 1,570 employees in 24 branch offices. Its paper-based loan document filing system got so massive that the bank had to add special structural supports to keep its building erect.

For a permanent solution to its paper problem, Banco Hipotecarios decided to electronically convert over 30 million of its paper loan documents into electronic images. To do this, 15 employees are working eight-hour shifts to prepare and scan an average of 100,000 documents (5–7 GB) each day. Documents are scanned into six Kodak 3500 Duplex scanners, which are preset for particular types of documents to accelerate the capture process using applications from local integrator, File Solutions SA.

Once scanned and indexed, the documents are inspected by QA representatives from File Solutions SA and are then stored in the bank's Informix Dynamic Server database using KOM's OptiStorm optical software. The documents are managed and made accessible to users through Westbrook Technologies' Fortis client-server document management software, custom designed to interface with the Informix database.

With this system, the information contained in the loan records (about 120–140 pages each) is instantly available at users' desktops for customer inquiries or internal communications. By plugging document management technology into its existing records database, the bank is reducing the paper piles in its offices and accelerating in-house data processing and customer service delivery, according to Juan del Rio, Banco Hipotecarios's system manager. Moreover, he added, the electronic retrieval and management of loan information is "bringing a greater level of organization, productivity, and efficiency throughout the institution."

2.3.4 The utility solution

British utility Essex and Suffolk Water [7] is improving service reviews and events to its customers with a new initiative supported by document opinions imaging and management technologies. Essex supplies drinking water to nearly 2 million commercial and residential customers. Historically, Essex service centers would manually route, count, and prioritize work using a microfilm-based archive system, which could not provide the speedy responses customers now expect from modern call centers. Essex also must continuously strive to meet strict quality and service standards set by OFWAT, the industry regulatory body. "We're swamped with paper," said Graham Gander, Essex's customer information manager. "It is very difficult for us to meet our standards of service in these circumstances."

To automate its customer correspondence processes, Essex has created Retrieving Information Via Electronic Routing Systems (RIVERS), a case management system based on Tower Technology's imaging and workflow technology. Incoming correspondence is now scanned, indexed, and routed to relevant customer teams, where workers can electronically access information from a customer's complete case history.

With the new system, Essex can respond faster and with better quality to customers' inquiries the day they are received, leading to fewer call-backs and increased productivity. "With better control of paperwork we can respond to customers' queries on their first contact," said Gander. RIVERS also lets managers access in real time information about outstanding work and individual staff productivity, which will help improve operational performance while addressing regulatory obligations.

Essex workers are adapting well to the new paperless system, according to Gander. "They don't see the need for paper at all anymore." While the system is expected to expand beyond the initial two departments, Gander said that the main benefits will be realized by Essex's customers. "This electronic system enables us to provide best-in-the-business customer service," he said.

2.4 The moving parts of DIM

Let's look briefly at the necessary "moving parts" involved in a document imaging and management system. Those familiar with the data communication and the computing world will see many of the same devices and systems necessary for a corporate network. Although there are many similarities to a common data network, there are also many differences.

The requirements to create, store, manipulate, and retrieve document images place unique demands on the system and generally raise the data network bar a few notches. The volume and characteristics of data that are dealt with create the need for different storage devices, higher-speed networks, and more accurate displays. These unique characteristics of DIM will be highlighted.

There are many "moving parts" required for a document and imaging system. These moving parts, the technology if we may, are the infrastructure and the necessary components needed to assure that the goals of DIM are met. In concept, there are six basic systems that comprise the moving parts of a DIM system. They are as follows:

1. Input system;

2. Display system;

3. Storage system;

4. Communication and network systems;

5. Printing and output systems;

6. DIM controlling software.

Figure 2.3 illustrates these systems. Each of these will be explained more fully in the following text.

As we begin the transformation of a paper document into an electronic image, we need an input system. The input system, also known as the document capture system, provides for the capture of a paper document for storage and processing within an electronic imaging system.

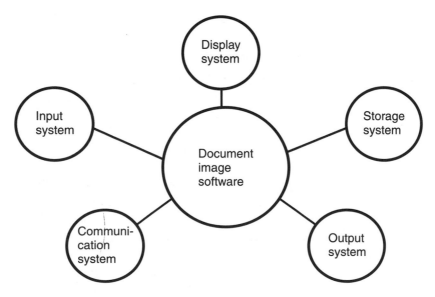

Figure 2.3   Systems of DIM.

The main moving parts within this system involve scanners, interfaces, and the necessary cabling. On the software side are elements to control the scanner, provide data extraction, and provide for indexing so the images can be properly retrieved. During the document capture process there are many steps to be done.

2.4.1 Preparing the documents

The first step involves preparing the documents for capture. Not all documents need to be scanned, so the first step would involve selection, movement, labeling, and repair for all documents deemed appropriate to be in the DIM system. Depending on the age and past storage characteristics of the document, the preparation stage can be lengthy. Often retroactive conversion, which involves capture of past records, is necessary for a DIM system to be fully functional. Other times this is done from a current point of time forward. Which conversion method used is a business decision that needs to be made based on corporate goals.

After the documents are readied for capture, they are run through a scanning phase, and, if necessary, as usually is, the images are enhanced (such as edge detection, speckle removal, rotation) to make up for deficiencies and transformation of the paper record. Following this, the data on the paper record (now an electronic image) are extracted via indexing (character representation of the image) or optical character recognition (OCR). This is necessary, since data on the electronic image are inherently not recognizable to the computer database and must be put into a recognizable form. Following indexing, the electronic image is ready for release into the DIM system for later use by office personnel.

The second system necessary for a DIM installation is the display system. The display system allows people, whether near or far away, to view and access the electronic document images. Components of this system consist of computer monitors, controller boards, and the necessary cabling. Due to the highly complex nature of the visual images, and the extended time periods that personnel are viewing these images, unique characteristics need to be considered.

Typical monitor features that need to be considered, based on the images being viewed, are color versus monochrome, display size, video output, resolution, and glare resistance of the screen. The monitor characteristics need to be matched closely with the controller boards' capabilities in resolution, refresh rate, flip rate, decompression algorithms, and bus support.

The final outcome is the requisite performance of the monitoring system as judged by the speed of image refresh rate and the quality (readability) of image. Typically, hardware components, under the guise of controller boards, are necessary to bring a normal PC workstation up to par to meet the unique needs of a document and imaging system.

2.4.2   The software

Closely coupled with the display and controller board is the image viewing software. Often part of the master DIM software, this provides the user with the ability to correct and enhance the image on the screen; annotate the electronic image, as one would annotate a paper document; manipulate the image (pan, zoom, and scroll); and display multiple pages. A typical current system would use a Web interface to provide this control. These elements, if properly selected, provide the speed, resolution, and features that are necessary to work in a document image capacity.

The third necessary moving part of a DIM system is the storage system. These devices, drives, media, and interfaces are necessary to manage the storage of imaged data through the life cycle of the document. But the characteristics of DIM put many strains and requirements on a storage system. To store a single page of word processed text may take up 8 KB of data storage, while an image of the same page, uncompressed, will require 1 MB of storage!

It is an order of magnitude different for storage and manipulating these electronic images and therefore whole new storage systems have been created. To select an appropriate storage system three variables need attention—speed of retrieval, cost, and capacity. While RAM storage provides excellent speed, it comes at a very high cost and is therefore limited in capacity. Removable media, such as Zip disks, provide for capacity at an effective cost but trade this for speed of data transfer. The optical drive, with an attached jukebox, provides the optimum cost, speed, and capacity environment for DIM. These optical drives and requisite jukeboxes handle the many disks and allow for the voluminous storage needs of organizations.

Another consideration related to storage is where, logically, to put the images. The choices come in on-line, near-line, far-line, and off-line storage mechanisms. As we move farther from on-line storage, data become slower to pull but cheaper to store. Again, business decisions on where to put data, usually based on age of data and frequency of retrieval, dictate how the image is stored logically.

Another facet of storage that needs consideration is image lifetime. All media, even paper, have a life span. Legal considerations and business needs usually guide this decision, but it must be considered so that the electronic images do not age out. Be aware that image lifetime consists of both media and technology life span. For example, eight-track storage of our music may still be existent on the tape itself, but without a working player, those data on the cassette are useless.

2.4.3   Developing the network

The fourth necessity for DIM is the communications and networking system. The communication system allows users to be at a distance from the image storage and management devices and allows for the retrieval of data on an entire campus, in the city, or, because of the prevalence of the Web, in the world. A document imaging system puts unusual and additional strains and requirements on networks.

This data flow goes from image creation, to storage devices, down to, upon request, a display screen on a user's workstation. The flow of information is measured in megabytes, and the user will typically demand instant response time. This often requires network segmentation, network monitoring, a fast backbone, and logical placement of the devices so that the enterprise network will not be stressed. Almost always, the current network will require upgrading to support the needs of a document imaging system.

With wide-scale company implementation, the Web is often used as the communication system. Fortunately, most DIM software is developed with a Web-enabled interface, so access from afar is possible. The speed and reliability of the Web often become factors in this equation, but there are technologies present that can attenuate this issue.

The fifth moving part of a DIM system is the printing and output system. This system includes hardware, software, and interfaces required to produce a hard copy, generally on paper, so that it can be accessed independently from the imaging system. Maybe in years to come images will not have to be transferred back into a paper format, but given our current environment, and the lack of a universal electronic medium, it is safe to say that paper will be a common denominator.

In order to provide this feature, printer selection, connection speed, and accelerator boards are issues that need consideration. Other variables to consider include additional memory to form the images onto paper, printer types (laser, ink jet), and the printing format that the DIM package will use (such as PostScript or metacode).

The glue that binds these systems together is the document imaging and management software. These software packages contain the storage software, the image viewing software, and the database and will allow the organization to control the work flow of the images throughout the organization. Based on the hardware in the previous five systems, the DIM software integrates the disparate elements into a business application. Software ranges from desktop small-user solutions to enterprise solutions and complex entities. Vendors and products in the field can be gleaned from magazines and professional organizations.

2.5   Questions to be answered

Although the technological tools are important, the real success of DIM comes only from people. In order to successfully implement a DIM system the following questions must be answered:

Strategy—How does the organization work or how does the upper management want it to work?

Process—What is the impact on the organization and people of the current process and the planned process? (In this arena work flow is studied in depth.)

Capability—Once agreement has been reached regarding the strategy and planned process, what capabilities are required?

Tools—What are the proper technological tools to make the strategy come into being?

In an artificial world, the aforementioned arenas would be brainstormed and agreed to by management for implementation. But in the real world many factors affect these elements. Factors such as regulatory concerns, stockholders, employees, customers, and suppliers all add requirements and direction. These four elements are the foundation for a DIM system, and agreements and compromises must be made to make a successful implementation.

2.6 Professionalism in the field

As mature fields, document imaging and management have professional organizations and certification bureaus to assist in maintaining and promoting professionalism. In the DIM field, probably the most recognized certification that one can obtain is that of a certified document imaging architect (CDIA). The CDIA is a nationally recognized credential acknowledging competency and professionalism in the document imaging industry.

CDIAs pose critical knowledge of all major areas and technologies used to plan, design, and specify an imaging system. The CDIA exam, although developed by a team of industry experts, is vendor neutral in its application and testing. As with most corporate certifications it is a consistent, objective way to evaluate imaging industry professionals. A majority of requests for proposals and second-level hires in the DIM field require a CDIA certification. Additional details and sample exam questions can be found at www.comtia.org.

Up the ladder from the CDIA certification are the MIT (Master of Information Technology) and Laureate recognition. Details on these recognitions and their requirements can be gleaned from the Association of Information and Image Management (AIIM) site [8]. The field also has many professional organizations and magazines that coordinate, disseminate, and analyze information for the field. Of the many professional organizations, AIIM is the largest and most respected. It provides a yearly national conference that attracts thousands of people and sponsors many regional conferences aligned to meet local needs.

2.7 Conclusion

The field of document imaging and management is growing and changing. One obvious sign of this change is the adoption of KM as the overarching umbrella under which DIM resides. One of the leading trade magazines has even adjusted its name and related national conference to reflect the strategic adjustment to KM. The projection of 25% to 30% growth per year for the next five years highlights the field incorporation. The field of DIM is also growing.

The goal of enterprise document management systems (EDMS) is to tame the paper tiger and to do more with less. Getting a firm grip on records and documents has bewitched enterprises for over 100 years. Much attention is being paid to the creation and management of structured electronic data, but the problems posed by the continuing onslaught of paper records still have not been overcome. In fact, the very tools that create the paper and electronic mountains have enhanced them. In most organizations, the management of records and other paper documents remains in a state of anarchy.

The solution to the problem is here. DIM, if properly implemented, can provide management of the process that informs and helps organizations. DIM systems do not assist only with the management of the media or the technology but with the management of information on the media. What is the payback for the implementation of DIM? Operational support, wider availability of information, faster and more local response to document queries, ability to reduce duplication and storage, and the ability to reduce costs and therefore increase profits. But the implementation of DIM is not just the implementation of the requisite technology. It is the adoption of change. As Abraham Lincoln once said, "The dogma of the quiet past are inadequate to support the present . . . as our case is new, so we must think anew and act new."

References

[1]   Gartner Group Inc., 56 Top Gallant Road, Stamford, CT 06904.

[2]   www.aep.com

[3]   Crowe, Chizek and Company LLP, 330 East Jefferson Boulevard., P.O. Box 7, South Bend, IN 46624-0007.

[4]   www.peoplesoft.com

[5]   KMWorld On-line, January 10, 2000.

[6]   KMWorld On-line, February 25, 1999.

[7]   KMWorld On-line, July 26, 1999.

[8]   www.aiim.org

CHAPTER

3

Groupware: messaging and cooperation

Philip D. Campbell

3.1 Introduction

Groups of people have needed to work together throughout history—organizations that solve the manifold problems of group cooperation succeed and those that don't fail. In recent decades the successive advent of the mainframe computer, the desktop personal computer, and networks of personal computers has allowed the development of many creative new tools to allow people to work together to solve their common problems. We call these tools groupware.

Groupware is a term that carries several definitions, the most formal of which come from the academic world. The study of computerized systems that enhance the work of groups of people is called Computer-Supported Cooperative Work, or CSCW [1]. One definition of groupware is the implementation of CSCW concepts and methods.

In the most narrow and perhaps most common definition, groupware is one of a fairly small number of software suites designed to be used and marketed as tools to enhance group work. Lotus Notes, Microsoft Exchange, Novell GroupWise, and Netscape Collabra dominate the market of groupware products.

In the broadest sense, groupware is any computer software product intended to enhance the ability of coworkers to work together. Many products fall under this definition that are not expressly marketed as groupware. E-mail systems, electronic bulletin boards, and the Internet itself, for example, are not often marketed as groupware, although all enhance group work.

3.2   A wide view

In this chapter, we take a wide view of groupware. We're concerned with computer-mediated sharing of knowledge among members of groups and much less interested in whether or not the software being used is or is not officially groupware. The wide view encompasses many, many software products, which can be sorted and classified in a number of ways.

EMS instant messaging	Chat Instant messaging Video conferencing EMS Application sharing	Simultaneous (synchronous)
		Interaction timing
E-mail Voice mail Discussion boards News groups Scheduling Calendaring	E-mail Voice mail Discussion boards News groups Scheduling Calendaring	Different times (asynchronous)
Same place	Different place	

Interaction
locale

Figure 3.1   Groupware classification by degree of separation.

A worthwhile question to ask when considering groupware tools is whether the members of the group work in the same or different places and whether they work at the same or different times. Groupware products can be sensibly grouped by the timing and location of their work, as illustrated in Figure 3.1. Coworkers whose work is asynchronous—that is, taking place at different times—have similar needs whether they work in the same or different places, as shown in Figure 3.1. Coworkers, whose work is synchronous are in the same place at the same time.

Any practicing businessperson can relate to every quadrant in Figure 3.1. All of these software tools and groupware techniques address familiar problems: ineffective meetings, telecommuting coworkers who rarely visit the office, team members with disparate schedules, and team members working in different time zones for different companies. It's not likely that any real company uses every technique to combat these problems, but it's equally unlikely that there is any modern company that uses none.

3.2.1 Groupware, the Internet, your intranet

The relationship between groupware and the Internet is a complex one that is still evolving as product vendors introduce new offerings and the marketplace sorts out what is important and what is valuable. The Internet and corporate intranets are ways of moving electronic information from one place to another and, as such, are important tools for group collaboration. Many companies use the tools of the Internet to disseminate documents internally. Such things as employee manuals and policy books are readily available on-line. Forms of all sorts—from tax tables to vacation requests to expense reimbursement requests—can be obtained 24 hours a day every day. Company newsletters and telephone directories are available at a mouse click.

Groupware can, and often does, use Internet technology without using any of the familiar Internet tools, such as Web browsers. The ubiquity of the browser, its affordability, and its user familiarity has made it an attractive part of many groupware implementation strategies.

3.2.2 Client-server architecture

Groupware systems are generally implemented as client-server systems. Individual users run software clients on their own personal computers. These clients communicate with server software, commonly via LANs or other networks. The client performs the human interface functions, allowing user input and displaying information for the user. The server provides coordination and communication among clients. Many tasks can be performed by the server or by the client. For example, the spell checker software in an e-mail system could, in principle, run on either the client or the server.

The proper division of functions between client and server is an ongoing issue in the groupware marketplace—different companies will find their needs best met by different blends of client and server. "Thin client" systems shift work to the server and rely on the client for minimal functionality. Centralization of functionality allows centralization of expense. "Thick client" systems shift work to the client, allowing more user autonomy. Thin client systems require more client-to-server communication than thick client systems. Our hypothetical server-based spell checker would require that the thin client transmit all the text to be checked to the server.

"Messaging" is the term for transfer of discrete messages between client and servers and among servers and is enabling technology for many groupware tools. Messaging is distinct from e-mail or any other specific application, since the message itself may not be seen or recognized by the user. For example, a message that is notification of a rescheduled meeting may be discernable to the user only as a change in a calendar display.

3.2.3   Groupware functions: e-mail

3.2.3.1   Overview

E-mail, or electronic mail, is a system that allows users to write text messages, conveys those messages to the intended recipient, and displays the messages to the recipient. Years of product competition have brought considerable enhancement and diversity to this seemingly basic function. E-mail is certainly the oldest, most widespread form of collaboration software, first implemented in the traditional mainframe environment and extended to the Internet at its inception.

It's hard to imagine a worthwhile groupware system without e-mail. The uses of e-mail are almost as numerous as its users. Travelers use it to keep in touch with the office. For telecommuters working at home it is a tool that is essential whether the office is across town or across the continent. It's used within small work groups, within huge divisions, between vendors and buyers. It is, in fact, increasingly difficult to imagine any business without e-mail.

E-mail has many obvious similarities to ordinary postal mail: addresses, mailing lists, replies, attachments, forwarding, "carbon copies," and even unwanted junk mail. All of these terms are used in ways that are recognizable from the traditional postal system and provide a feeling of familiarity for first-time e-mail users. There are significant differences, as well. When one sends an e-mail message, for example, there is no ink-on-paper signature, and special efforts are required to authenticate the identity of the sender. The postal system ends at your mailbox, but e-mail goes well beyond moving messages from one user to another. Incoming messages are stored together and there are tools to facilitate organization of and access to stored messages.

E-mail is not only part of all of the common groupware systems; a host of products is available from many vendors. Freeware products, such as Pegasus Mail, compete with products from software giants.

Early mainframe and LAN-based e-mail implementations were based on shared file storage. Each e-mail recipient has a section of disk storage that can be written into by message senders, but read only by the recipient. cc:Mail and Microsoft Mail are based on this architecture, which is being quickly displaced by client-server systems.

3.2.3.2 E-mail server functions

The e-mail server in a client-server implementation has several key functions, as illustrated in Figure 3.2. Since few e-mail users are willing or able to run their personal computers on-line all day, every day, practical e-mail requires central storage for messages. Such storage can be temporary, just until the client retrieves the messages, or it can be long term, including archival for later reference. The server component that performs this function is generally referred to as the message store.

There are two perspectives to message storage, based on viewing the client or the server as the primary storage site. One viewpoint is that the server provides temporary storage only and that messages are deleted from the server when they are downloaded to the client. It's then the responsibility of the user client to archive, save, or delete the message with concomitant responsibility to provide storage space, backup, and so forth. The second view is that server storage is primary. Messages are displayed by the client but generally not deleted from the server, which provides backup or archiving. As with many such seemingly dichotomous issues, there's no clear single answer for all companies, or even all users within a single enterprise.

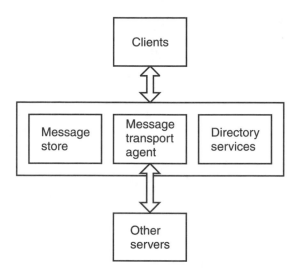

Figure 3.2   E-mail server block schematic.

Many companies, including Microsoft, Yahoo!, and others, operate free services in which mail is received and stored on a central server and accessed using an ordinary Web browser. Corporate use of these systems is restricted, but they illustrate the operation of centralized storage systems. Many software products can operate in server-oriented or client-oriented configurations, depending on user preference or corporate policy.

If e-mail is to be transmitted beyond the immediate work group, the server is required to transmit messages to other servers. The component of the server that accomplishes this is the message transport agent.

For security reasons, users must be authenticated when they send or receive mail through the server. Directory service is the component that performs this function, keeping track of users and groups of users, as well as their rights and capabilities. In addition, there may be directory information that is available to users and maintained centrally, such as a company directory that is available to all employees.

3.2.3.3   E-mail client functions

E-mail software clients are, of course, the portion of the system directly visible to users. Indeed, many casual users think of the client as their e-mail system. Standards for client-to-server and server-to-server interaction allow heterogeneous systems—two users can have clients from different manufacturers but use the same server. Different branches of an organization can have servers from different manufacturers that exchange mail. Indeed, were this not so, e-mail would not have achieved its near-universal status.

The chief functions of the e-mail client are to display and organize incoming messages and to allow convenient composition of outgoing messages. Most allow for easy reply to received messages and forwarding of messages to third parties.

3.2.3.4   Mailing lists

As with postal mail or corporate mail, e-mail users frequently need to send the same message to many recipients. Many e-mail clients allow the user to define distribution lists. The care of e-mail lists is labor intensive, especially when the list is long, subject to frequent change, or used by many senders. One solution is acquisition of specialized e-mail clients, designed expressly for maintenance and use of e-mail distribution lists.

These work well when both maintenance and use of the list are relatively centralized—for example, distribution of a monthly newsletter in a small company.

3.2.3.5   List servers

More problems occur when any member of a mailing list may want to send messages to the entire list. One strategy for dealing with large lists is the automated list server. In most cases, list members deal directly with the server software to join the list, update their own addresses, quit the list, inquire about addresses of other list members, and to send messages to the list membership. An administrator is still required, at minimum to deal with incorrect and obsolete addresses, but the maintenance load is substantially reduced. There are many variations, and maintenance of a busy or security-conscious list can require thoughtful sophistication.

When use of the list is restricted to a well-defined group of individuals, such as members of a project team or employees of a single company, the list is said to be closed and subscription is done or approved by the administrator. Members of the list may still send messages to the entire membership.

3.2.3.6   File attachments

There are many methods for moving information from one computer to another, each with its own virtues. E-mail provides a commonly used method for transmission of a file: the file attachment. Attaching a file to an e-mail message is especially practical for informal or one-time transmission of reasonably small amounts of data, especially if accompanied by discussion or commentary in the body of the message.

3.2.3.7 Filtering and electronic junk mail

E-mail boxes, like postal mailboxes, often seem filled with unrequested, unwanted messages. Unfortunately, the same technology that allows corporate users to send e-mail to lists of users allows marketers of many types to bulk e-mail possible customers. Often termed "spam," such messages use up transmission bandwidth and storage space. Although it's easy to click the delete button, it's annoying. Anyone who's away from the office for any length of time can return to filled storage quotas and dozens of unwanted messages. E-mail systems can be set to automatically handle various classes of messages differently if they can decide which messages belong to which classes, a process called filtering.

Software typically examines the address of the message sender, the text of the message body, and/or the text of the message subject for clues that a message is unwanted. Unwanted messages can be deleted or sorted into a special folder for later examination. Filtering can be done by the server or by the client. Server-based filtering can prevent every employee in a company from receiving the same electronic junk mail. Filtering also allows a user to sort less urgent e-mail into a separate area for later reading or to be alerted to a message from selected senders.

3.2.3.8 Message archival

Whether, when, and how to archive e-mail messages are difficult questions confronting system administrators. A busy company can process many thousands of messages daily, the vast majority of which have only ephemeral interest. Some may later prove to be important, even to the point of being legal evidence in litigation. At the time of a message's transmittal, it may not be evident whether it's of fleeting or enduring, critical importance.

3.2.3.9 E-mail issues to consider

The undisputed utility of e-mail has brought about its use in almost every corner of corporate life. Different uses in different corporate environments bring about a variety of concerns for corporate policy makers and e-mail administrators.

Users and administrators alike worry about the security and confidentiality of e-mail. It can be made as secure as desired, but added levels of security require user accommodation. Confidentiality of corporate e-mail, which legally belongs to the company, is more of a corporate policy issue than a technical issue. Some companies are concerned about the use and abuse of e-mail in ways that hurt the company, ranging from electronic sexual harassment to simple goofing off. Enterprises that merge or have relatively independent divisions sensibly worry about software communication standards and whether, and how, to standardize on an e-mail vendor.

3.2.4 Groupware functions: scheduling and calendaring

3.2.4.1 Overview

Few and fortunate are those who have not spent time struggling with coworkers in an attempt to find a mutually acceptable time for a meeting and a location in which to hold the meeting, once scheduled. Although groupware's goal is to make electronic collaboration more productive, face-to-face meetings are still an important part of the business scene. Simple e-mail may make the back and forth scheduling effort less time consuming, but it is nonetheless an onerous, frustrating task.

Many people use standalone calendaring software, an electronic analog to the paper day planner. Calendaring—a grammatically suspect, but standard, term—is tracking the activity of people and other singular resources over time: who's doing what at any given moment and who can access or change whose calendars. It's a relatively easy step to publish this information so that members of the group can see one another's calendar. Typically, there are degrees of sharing: A manager's secretary may have explicit access to the manager's calendar, including the right to make changes, whereas subordinates may see only when the boss is busy or free, in town or out of town.

Conference rooms, video conference equipment, and other facilities are often treated similarly meeting participants. Each piece of equipment has a calendar, and one person or a limited number of people have the right to schedule the calendar.

Someone needing to schedule a meeting can compare the meeting attendees' calendars to find a mutually available time and place, eliminating a major problem in traditional meeting scheduling. Messages are then exchanged between the scheduler and the meeting attendees, who can choose to accept or reject the meeting. The software can track tentative acceptances and prioritization of meetings.

Calendaring and scheduling, although intimately related, are not actually synonymous terms. Scheduling is the process of negotiating and arranging group activity [2]. Of course, manual scheduling of meetings is aided by calendaring software. Software designed to perform scheduling can actively take over the tasks of comparing calendars.

People issues are important for this function. Implementation is sometimes controversial—users fear their productive unscheduled time will be eaten by meetings and that managers will unilaterally schedule meetings from above. Many people dislike making their calendars visible.

3.2.5   Groupware functions: real-time conferencing

3.2.5.1   Chat and real-time text messaging
Chat systems are systems that are similar to e-mail in that the sender types text messages to be read by the recipient. The difference is that the sender and recipient are actively engaged at the same time and alternate in those roles in a conversation-like manner. Many products support on-line chat—for example, Microsoft's MSN Messenger, AOL, and ICQ.

Instant messaging is the ability to send brief one-way messages. AOL and ICQ are prominent providers. As the older analog cellular telephone system is phased out in favor of more modern digital systems, instant messaging through the mobile phone system will become readily available.

In both cases, the messages are seen as ephemeral, are rarely saved, do not include attachments, and are transmitted without formatting information. Indeed, they are often transmitted with marginal grammar and no punctuation.

Often viewed as merely the quintessential tool for teen gossip, real-time messaging fills a useful role in providing time-sensitive coordination, such as last-minute changes to a meeting location or agenda and travel coordination.

3.2.5.2   Audio conferencing
The telephone remains an important collaborative tool, although rarely considered part of a groupware suite, and its simultaneous use by more than two parties is an audio conference. Most corporate telephone systems support on-demand conferencing for a small number of participants. If more than a few parties are involved, special equipment is

required—a conference bridge provides the electronic connectivity for multiple parties and may usefully automate the process of establishing the conference. The major telephone companies provide bridging services, as well.

3.2.5.3 Video conferencing

Visual clues are important for personal communication, but travel for face-to-face meetings is expensive. Video conferencing, which allows use of visual information at much less cost than travel, is increasingly accessible for many companies. The introduction of improved video compression techniques and lower transmission costs have made video conferencing less expensive, but it hasn't reached the corporate mainstream in the way its enthusiasts have predicted [3].

3.2.5.4 Electronic meeting support

Meetings are a notoriously inefficient collaborative technique. Everyone has endured meetings in which many words were spoken but little was said, meetings dominated by a few speakers, and meetings that were recalled very differently by different participants.

Electronic meeting support (EMS) systems are systems designed to improve the efficiency of meetings, whether the participants are together or geographically distributed. Typically participants use a keyboard to enter their contributions as text and a trained facilitator mediates the session.

EMS systems avoid many of the factors that make face-to-face meetings ineffective: domination by a few individuals, management rank-pulling, fear of criticism, and simple shyness. The facilitator assures everyone an equal opportunity to contribute. Participation is usually anonymous, so participants are more willing to be honest and ideas can be evaluated independently of their contributor. EMS systems have significant down sides as well: the equipment and facilitator are expensive. More importantly, many corporate cultures are not ready for frank and honest expressions of opinion [4,5].

3.2.5.5 Application sharing

Application sharing is an adjunct to real-time conferencing in which several parties share a software application, such as word processing or drawing. Typically used in conjunction with an audio conference or chat, the parties alternate or vie for control of the software. Engineers discussing a drawing may find it useful to alternate control of a pointer or drawing tool to augment the audio conversation.

3.2.6 Groupware functions: asynchronous conferencing

3.2.6.1 Voice mail

Voice mail is a system that gives telephone callers who have not reached the desired party a chance to leave a recorded message that will be retrieved by the recipient at a later time. System vendors have given corporate users a rich variety of products, ranging from simple answering-machine-like functionality to sophisticated systems integrated with newer telephone systems and their feature-rich proprietary telephones.

3.2.6.2 Bulletin boards, newsgroups, discussion boards

There has always been a need for one-to-many communication. An e-mail user can send the same e-mail message to many people, but this requires specification of the precise recipient list. List servers allow implicit specification, but the messages flow with no organized structure. The time-honored office bulletin board has its electronic analogs and, as with e-mail, the electronic version has many properties that go well beyond the old bulletin board of paper and pushpins. Bulletin boards and discussion boards are essentially synonymous and generic. The term "newsgroup" is specific to Usenet, an Internet mechanism for organizing and distributing informational postings.

One useful aspect of discussion boards is their hierarchical organization. Once a topic is broached, sometimes by an administrator or organizer, users respond to already posted messages. Since a single posting can have many replies but is itself the reply to a single message, the overall structure takes on a hierarchical structure called a tree, as shown in Figure 3.3. Messages can be sorted by date or by posting user, but the tree structure provides a powerful tool for grouping messages by topic with minimal centralized effort. Unlike e-mail, the messages are stored centrally and newcomers to the board can view past messages.

Many technical companies find that product-specific discussion boards provide an invaluable tool in communication with and among customers. Users can ask and answer product questions, discuss prospective product developments, and benefit directly from one another's experience with the product. Vendor employees can gauge the state of their user community by reading the postings. Some vendors choose to participate in the discussion; some do not. If the vendor does not openly

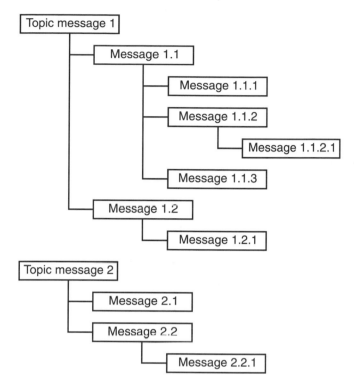

Figure 3.3 Hierarchical organization of discussion group postings.

participate, users will suspect that some of their fellows are company surrogates or undercover employees.

3.2.6.3 Unified messaging

A single individual may send, receive, and accumulate messages in a variety of formats or media: e-mail, fax, voice mail. Most commonly, they are dealt with by using separate software tools. There is a growing realization that a single tool for multiple media presents substantial advantages.

Messages in several media can be correlated. For example, you might want to send a voice mail message to provide an explanation of a forwarded e-mail. You might want to reply to a fax via e-mail. You may want to list all your messages from a particular sender chronologically.

The e-mail user interface is a much better tool for managing messages than the standard voice mail telephone interface. If the message server is sufficiently integrated with the telephone system, it is possible to use one computer interface for all messages.

Unified messaging is available, but still uncommon. It requires an unusual amount of systems integration expertise and expense, since different vendors frequently provide the telephone system, the voice mail system, and the e-mail system.

3.2.6.4   Messaging standards

It's a commonly observed aphorism that one nice thing about computer standards is that there are so many of them to choose from. The unknown wag who first made this observation would surely point to groupware and its components as a model. Product vendors devise and adopt standards even as they seek product differentiation.

In the heyday of the mainframe, hardware vendors developed proprietary methods for terminal-to-computer and computer-to-computer communication. In the era of proprietary, relatively isolated LANs, the contenders developed proprietary messaging standards. Efforts to build bridges between systems yielded further standards. In the 1990s, the techniques of the Internet and its TCP/IP networks have firmly established themselves in the marketplace, and systems based on these standards are supplanting older systems.

3.2.6.5   Internet messaging: HTTP, HTML, NNTP

Hypertext Transport Protocol (HTTP) and Hypertext Markup Language (HTML) are the key protocols of the World Wide Web. The former specifies how Web pages are transported from the remote site to the browser for display, and the latter describes the encoding of information within Web pages themselves. Network News Transport Protocol (NNTP) standardizes transport of Usenet news information.

3.2.6.6   E-mail client to server: POP3, IMAP4, HTTP/HTML

Post Office Protocol 3 (POP3) and its successor, Internet Message Access Protocol 4 (IMAP4), specify the interaction of client and server when they are linked by a TCP/IP network, as shown in Figure 3.4. This is a very common arrangement, especially in heterogeneous networks. These protocols perform client authentication and transfer of messages. IMAP is a significant improvement over POP, including encrypted security transactions between client and server. A single server can serve both POP and IMAP clients.

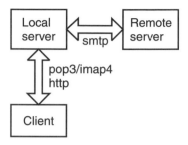

Figure 3.4 TCP/IP protocols for e-mail.

A relatively recent development is use of Web browsers as e-mail client's client. In this scheme, the user runs an ordinary browser to access an Internet or intranet Web site using the ordinary HTTP protocol. E-mail server software at the Web site formats the e-mail messages as Web pages for display at the user computer, using HTML. This is a thin client strategy, since the server stores messages, organizes messages, and maintains any recipient lists. An advantage to this strategy is that the e-mail is accessible from any Web connection anywhere in the world. A disadvantage is that browser interfaces are relatively feature poor.

3.2.6.7 Server-to-server: X.400, SMTP
X.400 is an international standard for exchanging messages between disparate systems; it is still in use in large organizations that make use of proprietary systems. The explosive growth of the Internet has propelled its Simple Mail Transfer Protocol (SMTP) to almost universal use.

3.2.6.8 Directory services: X.500, DNS, LDAP
The large-scale e-mail system of servers exchanging mail depends on transmitting servers being able to identify the correct server for each message and for conveying the identity of the proper recipient to the receiving server. X.500 is an international standard for exchange of directory information. A relatively recent development, X.500 is a complex system that organizes recipients hierarchically.

The Domain Name System (DNS) is the familiar scheme in which Internet host computers are specified as host.companyname.com and e-mail addresses are username@companyname.com. The Lightweight Directory Access Protocol (LDAP) has been endorsed by several e-mail vendors to achieve some of the sophistication of X.500 and the simplicity of DNS.

3.2.6.9   Data encoding: MIME

There is more to sending e-mail messages than transmitting text. It's desirable to be able to format the message's appearance by specifying the placement, color, size, and font of text or by embedding graphics. Further, attachments aren't necessarily simple text and can consist of formatted text, graphics, executable code, or any other computer file type. Multipurpose Internet Mail Extension (MIME) is commonly used for encoding nontext information within the message or its attachments.

3.2.6.10   Voice mail

Traditionally voice mail programs were implemented using either proprietary protocols or least-common-denominator signaling via telephone touch tones. In the former case the voice mail system tended to be very feature rich and easy to use but designed and sold strictly for a single telephone system. In the latter case, the voice mail could be used with almost any telephone system but was relatively unsophisticated and difficult to use.

Several standards for software interaction with telephone systems have arisen, most notably Microsoft's Telephony Application Programming Interface, TAPI, and Novell's Telephony Services Application Programming Interface, TSAPI. Each has attracted significant support among telephone system manufacturers, but voice mail based on proprietary protocols remains the most common.

3.2.6.11   Calendaring and scheduling

Several standards have been proposed with little market success. The Internet Engineering Task Force has sanctioned the Internet Calendaring and Scheduling Core Object Specification, ICAP, or iCalendar [6].

3.3   Conclusion

Lotus Notes, Microsoft Exchange, Novell GroupWise, and Netscape Collabra are topics of discussion in corporate circles as software has never been discussed before. Groupware tends to be a more personal thing for executives than COBOL or even BASIC. The techniques found under the broad umbrella of groupware are making a difference every day, even in companies that have no formal groupware strategy or policy. Some tools—email, voice mail, on-line discussion boards—are so widespread as to be an unnoticed feature of the corporate landscape. Others—electronic meeting support tools and automated scheduling—are much less common.

Systematic implementation of groupware within an enterprise represents a significant investment of funds and human effort. Many companies have received a rich return of increased productivity. Many have not. Frequently the distinction lies in the companies' differing willingness and ability to deal with the people issues the use of groupware raises [7]. Different groupware tools present different people issues. The same individuals who embrace e-mail and on-line discussion groups may resent calendaring and simply refuse to use scheduling.

In any case, careful thought is required to choose tools wisely and induce their acceptance among actual users. It's essential that users see that groupware use is not a passing fancy that will be abandoned by management when another fad hits the business press.

References

[1]   M. Pendergast, and S. Hayne, "Groupware and Social Networks: Will Life Ever Be the Same Again?" *Information and Software Technology* 41 (1999): 311.

[2]   C. Knudsen, and D. Wellington, "Calendaring and Scheduling: Managing the Enterprise's Most Valuable, Non-Renewable Resource—Time," in *Groupware: Collaborative Strategies for Corporate LANs and Intranets*, ed. D. Coleman, (Upper Saddle River, NJ: Prentice Hall, 1997), 115–141.

[3]   D. Chaffey, *Groupware, Workflow and Intranets: Reengineering the Enterprise with Collaborative Software* (Woburn, MA: Digital Press, 1998), 53–58.

[4]   J. Markowitz, "Using Meetingware and Facilitators: Guidelines and Case Studies," in *Groupware: Collaborative Strategies for Corporate LANs and Intranets*, ed. D. Coleman (Upper Saddle River, NJ: Prentice Hall, 1997), 255–265.

[5]   D. Chaffey, *Groupware, Workflow and Intranets: Reengineering the Enterprise with Collaborative Software* (Woburn, MA: Digital Press, 1998), 60–66.

[6]   D. Chaffey, *Groupware, Workflow and Intranets: Reengineering the Enterprise with Collaborative Software* (Woburn, MA: Digital Press, 1998), 70–72.

[7]   G. O'Dwyer, A. Giser, and E. Lovett, "Groupware & Reengineering: The Human Side of Change," in *Groupware: Collaborative Strategies for Corporate LANs and Intranets*, ed. D. Coleman (Upper Saddle River, NJ: Prentice Hall, 1997), 565–595.

CHAPTER

4

Contents

Developing effective knowledge with both qualitative and quantitative research

Steve Jones
Elia Diamadatou

4.1 Introduction

The value of qualitative data as information to be used for forecasting, assessing, and providing feedback for change in a system has been confirmed by copious research and has been traditionally represented by a number. Numbers are an easy way to compare what has been uncovered: 40 percent of the industry managers surveyed suggest they will change to Windows NT this year, seven out of ten mission-critical databases reside on a UNIX system, or the probability of high-speed wireless LAN networking in the 1,000 Mbps range by 2002 is less than 1 percent.

The value assigned to quantitative information is a tradeoff between providing a quick analytical representation of the information and an in-depth descriptive perspective of what the results represent. The importance of well-defined quantitative data to the field of KM is well recognized. The value of qualitative data used as information has not been as well defined.

Qualitative measurement techniques, including interviews, questionnaires, focus groups, Delphi analysis, rhetorical analysis, content analysis, and even ethnographic analysis, have gained popularity in the past 20 years. Yet still, there is a fundamental schism between quantitative and qualitative research methodologies. In reality they work best when they are blended together for a greater representation of the data. The rigor associated with qualitative analysis has long been challenged. However, when properly conducted, qualitative research becomes as powerful and as useful a tool as any analytical tool available.

4.1.1 Using quantitative and qualitative methods together for higher-quality data

The assumption that there is only one way to collect data is a myopic approach to the way we collect information in our day-to-day lives. We may read that a certain piece of telephony-related equipment might increase productivity within the network by 10%. Our first reaction would be to find someone who has used the product and will verify the claims put forth. By doing this, we mix the two approaches to find a clearer view of how the product actually performs.

By allowing both quantitative and qualitative methodologies to feed each other and help build an improved collection process we can illuminate the breath and depth of data gathered. An example would be to use focus groups to guide the development of surveys. The surveyed information may later support or refute the focus group results. This approach would widen the perspective of the research and allow the researcher to explore a new direction of information gathering more effectively than if just a singular method was employed.

Focusing on just one methodology will limit the perspective of the research. There are stories connected behind each survey item that may lead to a greater understanding of the product or service being evaluated. Quantitative methods are considered more objective in their approach, providing greater accuracy in data delivered based on the level of variables controlled (bias). Qualitative methods, whether they be specific (as interviews or more general such as focus groups), are designed to examine all variables in the context with each other, rather than sorting out a single component and attempting to be unbiased while examining it.

Qualitative methods are usually recommended for use in formative assessments, while quantitative methods are used most convincingly in summative evaluations.

It is also suggested that qualitative analysis can be used when detailed information is sought, the type that can only come from the dynamics associated with the interview, content analysis, focus group process, or the Delphi method. The Delphi method obtains a group judgment on an issue or a prediction. The researcher starts by selecting experts and getting them to answer a questionnaire or to make predictions and give their reasons (e.g., how will KM change in the future?). Their reactions are gathered in anonymous form and sent back to the experts with their previous answers indicated. The experts consider their colleagues' responses and decide whether and how to modify their own. A second round is similarly obtained and circulated for response. Usually three rounds suffice to get a sufficient combination of opinion.

Content analysis is a research technique for the objective and systematic description of the content of communication. The raw material for the research worker using the content analysis technique may be any form of communication, usually written materials, but other forms of communication, such as music, pictures, or even gestures, can be included. Content analysis is often used in conjunction with observational studies. The researcher usually tape records classroom verbal behavior, makes a typed transcript from the audiotape, and then analyzes the content of the transcript in order to measure variables that have been formulated by the researcher.

Guba and Lincoln [1] put forth a process that provides for a simple approach to gathering, analyzing, validating, and delivering qualitative data in a case report method. It is a multistep , process, which involves the following:

- Initiating a contractual relationship;
- Selecting and training the research team;
- Identifying all involved stakeholders;
- Looking for stakeholder perception of what claims, concerns, and issues they may have on the topic;
- Putting the claims into context;
- Finding consensus;

- Using other data analysis techniques, such as content analysis, ethnographic interviewing, or Delphi, to bring perceived constructions together with plans for resolution;

- Providing documentation and reiterations as necessary.

This entire process is used to research areas that cannot be "drilled down" effectively with standard quantitative methods. By digging deeply into the nature of the system, using alternative support data, and allowing for emergent themes to present themselves, the researcher can provide reliable data for the client or end user. Of course, the specific research determines which form of data gathering is to be used. Delphi and content analysis are tailored to specific questions or types of content, while the Guba/Lincoln methodology is general but can contain a variety of gathering techniques.

The dichotomy of quantitative versus qualitative is far from simplistic. Each method has its ardent supporters and detractors. Our goal is not to pose any philosophical positioning that would force the reader to choose one method over the other; rather it is to expose the researcher to an alternative approach to gather information in a reliable, trustworthy fashion that will yield valid data.

4.2   Problems

4.2.1   Pitfalls of qualitative measurements

The issues that arise from qualitative methods in research are primarily located in the processes of collecting and analyzing data concurrently. The researcher is positioned as the instrument to be used to collect the data—reflecting on a perspective that may be unique to the data collector. This close proximity of researcher to what is being researched leads to the arguments of contamination of the subject item. With the proper preparation, time, technique, and use of checks to validate the research reliable information can be gleaned.

Researchers establish general guidelines as to the direction that they expect their study to follow in qualitative analysis. But the need to leave open the possibility that these data may direct the researcher to follow a different path must remain flexible. Failing to keep a constant assessment of information gathered with respect to the research problem can result in missed opportunities, dead-end research, and limited significance of results once they are finalized.

Variability in subjects can be a considerable issue when using quantitative analysis. The representative sample is important to reduce the perceived effect of researcher bias. In qualitative research, there is a deliberate sampling performed in order to be opportunistic in obtaining information from the sources that are perceived to be the most abundant—this is called purposeful sampling. Purposeful sampling disregards the concerns of bias because its main goal is to gather information. Positioning the researcher such that each interview or observation will result in some useful information is a quick and direct avenue to data. Focus groups of homogeneous populations have been used for years as a method of obtaining current data on a select group that has the needed information for the researcher.

Another problem with qualitative measures is the time and expense involved in identifying, organizing, and classifying qualitative data. The advent of, and experience with, Web browsers and access techniques has helped greatly in recent years. Other chapters of this book will discuss the requirements for these activities and mention accessing, directory, and storage methodologies to help solve the problems.

Expert systems (an offshoot of artificial intelligence) were thought to be the solution to these problems. Although expert systems have been in development for over 30 years, there are still a number of open issues concerning their viability. Among these issues are some that are generally applicable to any data processing application and some that specifically apply to expert systems. The general issue is that all systems need to be maintained, updated, and modified over time as well as tested and validated.

Beyond these basics, expert systems have additional issues of scope. These include the difficulty of finding experts from which to abstract knowledge and the disappearance of experts and their knowledge either through death or decline of the knowledge. In addition to these burdens, there are a number of traditional difficulties with which those who wish to employ such a system should concern themselves.

There are structural issues as to how to design the system and what system platform to use. Moreover, there are also knowledge engineering issues regarding how to extract knowledge, codify it, enter it, merge it with other knowledge, and then how to test the operation of the system. Finally, there is the continued viability of the knowledge and its applicability to real problems. In addition to these warnings, the research practitioner should keep an awareness of the basic Boolean logic.

The most frequently employed form for storing knowledge in an expert system is one of storing a set of conditions that are subsequently tested in sequence. Based upon the results of the test, either one action or one of the other matching rules is executed.

An example of one of these rules is portrayed in the following instruction set:

```
IF "Condition 1 " occurs
   And IF "Condition 2 " occurs
      Then Perform Action 1, Action 2, . . . Action N
         Else Perform Action N+1, Action N+2, Action N+M
            End Test
```

Rule Structure

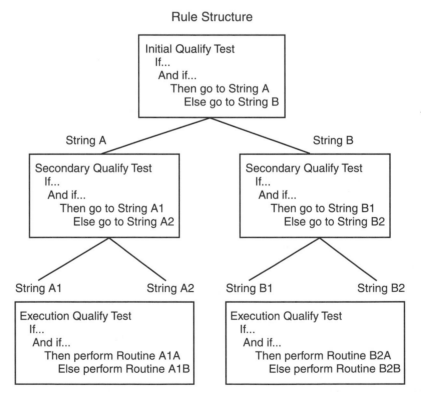

Figure 4.1   Example of storage of rules.

A sequence of such rule instruction sets can be further structured into a tree, such as that portrayed in Figure 4.1. Whether interpreted and stored in a computer or on a piece of paper, the researcher uses the same basic analysis methodology.

Charges of "guiding" the respondents' answers are sometimes leveled against qualitative research. Also, the researcher may be too close to the subject and cause a change in the environment being observed. Open-ended questioning is one of the hallmarks of qualitative analysis. By allowing the data to "emerge" from the process, the researcher allows for the free-flowing occurrence of important information that may (or may not) have a bearing on the topic being evaluated. By allowing the free-flow to occur and documenting the information accordingly, the researcher collects a database of tangential topics that are revisited to help solve the current issue or other issues that may be related to the research area.

4.3 Solutions

4.3.1 Providing reliable qualitative research

There are a number of ways to prevent charges of guiding, being too close, and limiting tangential concerns dominating data collection. The following is a list of procedures that should be constantly followed to ensure meaningfulness to the original intent of the assessment:

▸ Maintain the rigor of research and not rely too heavily on intuitive analysis.

▸ Be aware of alternative impressions of reality and varying outlooks that occur in the evaluation situation.

▸ Be aware of the various resources available to confirm primary sources of qualitative information—such as using observation and historical data to confirm interview data.

In any research, issues of validity and reliability define the applicability of the research. With qualitative assessment, these measures of the work quality are scrutinized with greater detail because of how data are gathered and analyzed. There are a number of ways in which these issues should be addressed.

Validity is displayed by conveying to the reader of the research the where, how, and why of gathering data.

Triangulation, gathering information from more than one source, will convey a check system of these data. Interviews, prolonged engagement of observation, and the collection of other artifacts balance the information from more than one material source.

Member checks, the process of feeding back to the participants the researcher's perception of the group's construction of the studied phenomena, are used to ensure that what was heard is actually what the participants thought they conveyed (misconceptions of emergent themes can be examined for any conceivable misinterpretations with this internal validity check).

The researcher's perceptions, balanced by member checks, can also be evaluated by peers to confirm the findings. Someone who is disconnected from what is being evaluated, but yet has an understanding of the research methodology, can be employed to make communication of the data understandable to the readers of the research.

Reliability of research makes the use of the results important to other related occurrences of similar issues. However, the qualitative approach to assessment does not depend upon the research itself to be generalizable to other conditions. It is incumbent upon the readers of the research to weigh the practicality of the work to their specific experiences. It is also the researcher's responsibility to convey with thick and rich description the context and conditions in which the assessment is conducted. With this descriptive audit trail, others may use the assessment as a template to their specific experience.

The credibility of the results and their acceptance may depend upon those who have commissioned the research to be performed. Quantitative results—hard and fast figures—are usually best met in an environment that is better suited for statistics and figures to evaluate conditions. However, when statistical positioning has the ability to sway the readership, a more thorough collection of information through qualitative means lends supportive data with relevant meaning to the statistical examination.

Providing the proper training to those who will be collecting qualitative data is critical. Similar perspectives must be shared when the researcher is the collection instrument of the data. By recording conversations and interviews, using checklists during the interview process, and cross-referencing gathered peer information with each researcher, a balance is maintained to ensure consistency in the way in which data are collected.

Collecting data in a qualitative methodology can be costly and time consuming. The researchers need to know what it is they are looking for and how to find it, rather than allow for wasted time in exploring these issues. If interviews are being used to collect data, then specific attention needs to be placed on keeping the interviewing environment free from any outside disturbances. Removing the interruptions associated with phone calls, office colleagues dropping by, or being surrounded by work that may need to be completed will allow the interviewing process to be more productive.

Recording data in a manner that can be reviewed and analyzed at a later time is critical to qualitative analysis. A tape recorder should be used to document the entire conversation. However, consent of the interviewee needs to be obtained in order to deliver an ethical research report. Handwritten notes to supplement the taped commentary should be used to add visual effects to these data. Observed conditions such as a displayed uneasiness by the interviewee or the inability to maintain eye contact throughout difficult questioning could add important insights when these data are reviewed and emergent themes are gleaned from the research. Transcription of the recorded conversations is important. The verbatim documentation of these data can be better analyzed for specific themes. One method used to analyze these transcribed data is to cut out the phrases or text that frequently occur during the interview. By matching the various groups of words, phrases, or text, certain patterns or consistencies are identified more easily.

Individual and group interview methods are used in qualitative research. Group dynamics have a way of bringing certain attitudes and responses to the surface that may otherwise not be uncovered. Groups can provide peer pressure and challenge the thought process of members to bring suppressed information to the fore. This "pressure" can also have a negative effect. It may cause the participant to retreat and refuse to contribute to the conversation. It is incumbent upon the researcher to guide this process and protect the integrity of participants so that the process does not unduly affect them. Ethical data collection needs to be supported with a full disclosure of intent to the participants—without any type of hidden agenda being held in abeyance from the participants.

Individual interviews should be used when data collection requires confidentiality of gathered information. It is extremely difficult to promise complete anonymity to the participants in this form of research. Care needs to be given to replace names, jobs, locations, and other easily correlated information so that the participant can be assured that what he or she divulges in relation to a sensitive topic cannot be used against him or her. Multiple perspectives (more than one researcher) need to be balanced in this effort also. Singular control of data flow is easier than multiple sources. Each researcher should be held to a strict code of not letting the data source be readily identifiable. Without providing this assurance, the participant may not be willing to open up and share information.

It is understood that most data gathered in a qualitative way may not be generalized to the larger sample from which these data were extracted. Qualitative measurements rely on the reader to provide meaning to the specific setting from the information delivered. It is incumbent upon the researcher to provide enough information about the setting in which the research was performed in order to give a meaningful relationship to the reader.

Case reports are used in this manner so that the reader can evaluate whether or not the setting described is similar to the type of situation in which he or she may be working. An example might be data collected on an IT project for a large family-owned corporation that is migrating to NT from a UNIX platform. The corporate locations may be spread out over a three-state area and encompass four different service providers. This type of detailed information can give the reader the context needed to see if the described data fit his or her specific business environment or are closely related to it.

4.3.2 Case study examples

The case study is used as a way to convey to the reader an in-depth examination with a unified perspective of environment, participants, and other variables in a singular report. Areas ranging from customer service in business-to-business markets to information technology use have been researched with qualitative analysis. Quality of service (QoS) issues in wireless technologies, which were previously defined by only statistical analysis of system error logs, have been enhanced by using qualitative methods to dig deeper into what makes the customer satisfied with the end product. Studies have also examined managerial and economic aspects of acquiring information technologies too quickly in an educational environment.

4.3.3 Quality of Service in the wireless industry

GTE Wireless [2] (now known as Verizon) has used an established perspective of how to define QoS. Coverage was considered the primary component of QoS. The footprint or the areas that the end user could travel in without paying roaming charges and feature consistency were second on the QoS list. The ability to be highly mobile was also regarded as important. All of these aspects could be quantified with regard to power output from the antenna, reception power received at the envelope edge, and how many calls were dropped during handoffs from one cell to another.

Today, carriers have taken a different view of what is important in bringing high levels of QoS to their customers. Evaluation is focused on the areas of service, quality (as defined by the customer), and price. Customers have come to expect more for less with greater roaming areas, more features, and seamless mobility provided as baseline services. How then would the perspective of the customer be evaluated to help reduce "churn," or the rate at which customers switch to other service providers?

GTE used a mixed method approach to deliver this information. By using traditional measures, such as dropped or lost call counts, system availability rates, and number of blocked calls, they evaluated the technology side of the services offered. On the user side of the equation they examined J. D. Powers surveys and user focus groups to glean data on satisfaction levels that are not defined by the technical competence of the network.

The study found that QoS is something that is defined by the customer, not by the engineering evaluations. Perceived quality can also be directly impacted by nonnetwork components, such as contact with a difficult customer service representative or inaccurate billing statements. The need to continually perform (the recycle stage) evaluations of the level of service should be part of the QoS plan.

By looking at these results, GTE realized that it was more cost effective to keep current customers satisfied with their service as opposed to going out and trying to find new customers to replace ones who had left because of dissatisfaction with their service. This information would have been painstakingly acquired by circulating numerous surveys in order to whittle down the various aspects that may have been important. Focus groups guided by the surveys helped the researchers to uncover and confirm the areas that end users were most concerned about.

4.3.4   Implementation of quick response information systems

Information to the floor in the retail industry has become important in the decision-making process associated with promotion, pricing, sourcing, and inventory management [3]. Information from these areas has become the third most critical resource in the retail industry along with capital investment and labor. However, the change of corporate culture, shifting work flows, political concerns, and organizational communications are all affected by the implementation of new technology to the showroom floor. The information delivery system, a quick response (QR) system, has been the medium used to provide this service.

Researchers developed a purposeful sample of the retail stores using a QR to best represent the different types of retail organizations. Data gathered were from in-depth interviews with the managers of the organizations that had implemented the systems. Though statistics of data input, inventory control, and other aspects of information management associated with the retail services could be used to calculate the efficiency of the system, the actual user satisfaction with the technology required use of the qualitative approach.

Power and political issues associated with the control of—and the loss of the control of—power were discovered. The change of perceived power related to who controls the information associated with the QR system was identified. The Management Information Systems (MIS) department had a perceived loss of power and a leveling of its importance to that of other support departments.

Organizational communication was enhanced in ways that required the managers to communicate across various departments and vendors—something that they had not done prior to the QR use. Territorial boundaries between MIS, accounting, customer service, and other areas were fused together because the information was now available to all units and not controlled by a single entity.

Workflow issues were also altered. Increased productivity in the form of less reordering, more time for customer service, and paying more attention to the delivery of products was noted. Without the qualitative inquiry, it would have been difficult to discover exactly the benefits of the implementation. An assumption could have been made with a questionnaire; however, if the wrong inquiries were made, no information would have been returned!

Corporate culture changes were issues that emerged from data, too. Resistance to change and where in the hierarchy of corporate structure the change affected dictated the acceptance of the QR system. Perverse effect, which occurs across all levels of corporate structure, was found to have the greatest resistance to the change. By using qualitative methods to discover these issues, future implementation of QR systems can be planned with these concerns anticipated.

4.3.5 Managerial and economic aspects of rapid information technology acquisition

Fairfield University had four unique questions concerning the use of computing technologies on its campus that would not be adequately answered by conventional quantitative methods associated with surveys and or use statistics [4]. The patterns of acquiring computing technologies and the perceived desires for computing needed to be examined on a level that could help the research plan more effectively for future requirements. Further examination of managerial issues directly related the influx of new information technologies also required examination.

Data collection, research questions, and the unit of analysis in qualitative research cannot be placed into a fixed mold as in experimental research, which makes it a target for commentary related to the lack of rigor associated with the methodology. However, this study used extensive collection points of information to draw its conclusions. Documentation, archival records, interviews, direct observations, and the physical artifacts (i.e., the technology acquired) were all considered and weighed for their importance and availability.

The conclusions and implications drawn from the extensive data collection process revealed differing perspectives of the importance of information technology (IT), priority levels of funding for new IT projects, the low confidence level of the infrastructure integrity, no formal procedure existing to define the servers using capacity planning procedures, and lowered user productivity due to resource allocation problems and other technology issues. The implications of these findings pointed to the need for budgeting information technology as a part of the institutional planning process, and that the planning cycle for implementing technology should be shortened to facilitate the institution's response rate to changing technologies that could enhance the teaching, learning, and administrative environment.

4.3.6 Client-server computing

Logan and Lutz [5] examined the literature related to client-server computing for data related to the dynamics of implementing the technology and what, if any, contribution qualitative analysis would provide in looking at the complex issues of social and organizational impacts resulting from new technology deployment. The dynamics of the client-server environment are constantly changing and should have research attached to the "what not to do" items in both quantitative and qualitative means.

Management information system professionals could be assisted in complex system upgrades and additions to legacy environments if they had historical data to reference. Knowledge, the microsocial processes of implementing new technology into the corporate environment, can be critical to transitioning into new applications, processes, and procedures. Disregarding the human element and prioritizing the technology in a client-server computing environment add additional, but avoidable, challenges to the installation process. Systematic research could reduce the conflicts from the human component associated with information technology.

4.4 What to do next: use new technology

Mentioned previously are the difficulties of identifying, organizing, and classifying qualitative data. In recent years many companies have developed technology to assist with these problems. Following are some of the products currently available to help. Use of these products could provide a great deal of qualitative information from external and internal sources.

> **BackWeb** (www.backweb.com)—"People don't have the time to go out and grab the new data, so we proactively provide critical knowledge," according to BackWeb. Given that goal, the company has five key tools that monitor connection for nonintrusive downloads, deliver data in packets, compress all files, only refresh changed data where possible, and stagger delivery to meet demand cycle. "We can create knowledge channels, just like we have file channels right now," states BackWeb. The company channel profilers automatically profile and filter channels and can set alerts for high-interest information.

Verity (www.verity.com)—Corporate power users want two things from a search program: a corporate Yahoo! and the same information available differently for different audiences. The value of such predictable categorization is rapid access to known resources. The same body of information should be parsed into different views and access security based on departments and need-to-know requirements. Access can be determined via log on and password. The goal is to take the best of document management and apply it unobtrusively with categorization systems that learn how users categorize files.

Open Text (www.opentext.com)—According to Open Text, "Information retrieval is an extremely limited view of KM. The process of creating knowledge includes sharing and using it. Context has everything to do with it. The question is how to make KM useful in business life." The goal is to learn from discussions that lead to decisions. Instead of searching for words or documents, a system is needed to find the tasks that are assigned to solve problems, to see the documents that are used, and to learn the success of project schedules. Open Text offers a system designed to take tacit knowledge, or to understand the way smart and effective people respond to problems and opportunities, and make this knowledge searchable.

4.5 Conclusion

Focusing on just one method of information gathering and analysis can leave serious holes in the data collected. By coordinating and bringing together both forms of research—qualitative and quantitative—results can provide a clearer picture of the topic examined. The qualitative methodology can be performed in a rigorous, trustworthy manner that can be relied upon for accurate representation of several situations. By giving attention to the various aspects associated with providing validity in a study, the reader of the research is given the opportunity to view a more three-dimensional or holistic analysis. Qualitative measurements can be used across disciplines and topics to provide more critical information and greater comprehension of the researched topic.

Further investigation and application of qualitative research into the human element of information technology deployment may give a different perspective about how system installations or upgrades could be handled and eliminate some of the user challenges associated with information technology.

The case study results demonstrate that modeling can be used to create effective marketing intelligence for use in competitive situations. It confirms that this intelligence can be developed in situations where the available data are less than perfect in their comprehensiveness and (statistical) reliability. Decision makers can be provided with directional information for current and emerging situations by managing the available information to capitalize on its combined predictive power. Modeling improved on intelligence that was based on only one type of data in earlier efforts, especially by providing guidance early in competitor entry.

Based on the case study results, decision makers facing competitive situations should be encouraged to welcome and consider any type of data that might be related to understanding customer and competitor activities. In fact, every type of data input in the modeling contributed, through some specific variables, to understanding drivers for churn. Decision makers should assess the value of using such diverse data against the appropriate in-market criteria, including measuring the predictive power of these data via data mining.

References

[1]   E. G. Guba, and Y. S. Lincoln, *Fourth Generation Evaluation* (Newbury Park, CA: Sage, 1989).

[2]   L. Rudolph, *GTE Wireless Quality of Service* (Richardson, TX: IEC Comforum, 1998).

[3]   A. Aldridge and A. L. Harris, "Implementing IT-Based Systems: Lessons from the Retail Industry," *Journal of Computer Information Systems* (Winter 1998/1999).

[4]   W. Trellis, "Introduction to Case Study," *The Qualitative Report* 3 (July 1997).

[5]   P. Y. Logan and C. M. Lutz, "Establishing the Research Foundations for Successful Client/Server Computing: What Naturalistic Studies Could Contribute," *The Qualitative Report* 4 (January 2000).

CHAPTER

5

Contents

Systems architecture: the preparation for KM

Richard F. Bellaver

5.1 Introduction

This chapter deals with the storage, identification, and quality of data. The emphasis is only on one aspect of the KM benefit spectrum—that of quality. But the emphasis on quality provides the requirements for several of the other topics explained in this book. The chapter also explains the detail data planning, as well as the corporate planning, that must take place for a company to derive any benefit from KM activities.

Besides attempting to optimize on new hardware and software, the phenomenon and the obsession with KM in American industry is having a profound effect on company IT planning. The practicality of distributed data processing (DP) and the desire to take advantage of the latest technology has led many companies to concentrate on cleaning up the databases and restructuring the processing. (Sometimes these things have been done just under the excuse of "reengineering.")

The twofold approach provides a challenge to both corporate IT and business planning communities. The difficulty for planners in attempting to get to KM is an apparent inconsistency in the "quality" definition in IT. Are the advertising descriptions of processing (e.g., new, improved, faster) in conflict with the historical descriptions of data (e.g., identifiable, complete, accurate)?

In those companies undergoing mergers or acquisitions, bringing together diverse IT systems, organizations, and methodologies provides an even more challenging opportunity. Even some of the large, more stable IT organizations have experienced the accordion effect of centralization versus decentralization leading to a similar "clean it up and make it better" situation.

A look at an evolution of the strategies concerning system architecture can be an aid to realizing the problems of getting ready for KM. Computer system architecture is the logical structure and relationship of the data and application functions used to satisfy a company's business requirements. There is a practical architectural technical evolution that can lead to quality-based data, but the nontechnical problems of sharing data for corporate advantage may be more severe than the technical.

Data can be a most valuable asset to a business, and technology can allow shared access to those data faster than ever. If the benefits of data mining are based on shared data, there should be no problem with the methodology being used by most present IT organizations. However, there must be a logical approach to the establishment of data quality procedures before the benefits of mining and warehousing can be attained. At a minimum, interdepartmental battles about ownership of data must be fought, new chargeback algorithms must be accepted, and managers will probably have to learn at least some new coding structures if not some new languages. An examination of the present systems of many companies will establish a base for comparison.

5.1.1 Current architecture

Even with the advent of client-server and unbridled growth in the use of PCs, the current architecture of many large computer systems can generally be defined as mainframe oriented, standalone, and data redundant. This situation did not happen by accident. The early approach to IT for most large companies was to search for projects based on economy of scale. For example, companies looked for large, team-sized applications.

Usually, for order clerks or bill investigators, manual training methods and procedures had been standardized to achieve the last measure of efficiency. Computer mechanization followed the model of these standard operating procedures.

Very large, organizational-oriented systems were built based on the need to increase operational productivity. Generally, the systems used for order processing, dispatching, billing, inventory control, financial control, and many other business functions have been developed using the most efficient technology for both hardware and software.

That technology in the past was basically large mainframes. (These systems are currently referred to as "legacy systems" with somewhat negative connotations. Notwithstanding that they did give us the Y2K problem, my experience is that the developers did the best they could with the ideas and the tools at hand and laid the groundwork for all that has followed.)

In many cases, a total systems approach to mechanization was implemented with that organizational orientation. All data needed to solve a business problem were isolated. The work groups that needed access to the mechanized process were identified, and the rules of the data, the processing, and the communications to solve the specific problem were defined and implemented into one system.

As depicted in Figure 5.1, if customer name was necessary to support system 1, it was acquired, edited, and stored. If these data were needed for system 2, they were also acquired, edited, and stored, but according to a new set of rules (maybe system 1 stored last name first then a comma and first name, while system 2 stored first name and then last name and no comma.) At best, these data were passed off-line from one to N, and then still edited according to system N rules and stored again, usually in a new format.

As a result of the magnitude of the process, the large volume of data, and the limitation of hardware and software capabilities, all aspects of each system were tightly integrated to ensure efficiency of processing time and data storage charges. The cost justification of the project was usually based on increasing human productivity. User departments that paid for the development and the use of the systems reduced cost by reducing human resources. User departments had a very proprietary interest in both the data and the supporting processing system.

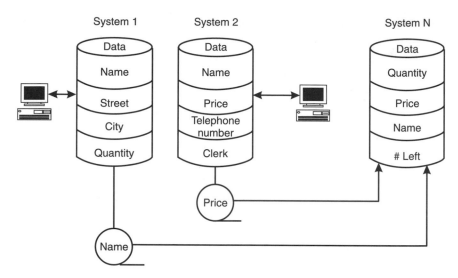

Figure 5.1 Current architecture.

The state of the art, especially the limitations of database management systems and communications software, also left its mark on the current architecture. In many cases, systems developed were efficient, monolithic, inflexible, end-to-end special-purpose procedure speeder-uppers owned by various departments. The computer implementations matched the work, the work matched the organizations, and a degree of stasis was obtained. However, over time, most organizations are subject to significant change.

To contain costs as a corporation moves forward (especially toward centralization or integration), there is a need to increase partnering of organizations, and sharing resources and data is required. Technology cost structure changes and user needs become more sophisticated. Unfortunately to meet this change, most current architectures are characterized by the following;

- ▸ Many large standalone systems with individual communications networks;

- ▸ Data configured differently for each process;

- ▸ Redundant functionality and data;

- Inability of organizations and systems to access other organizations' systems and data;

- A nonquality situation.

5.2 Problems: the opportunities and the challenges

The current architecture picture looks pretty bleak. Must everything be thrown out and started over to clean up and restructure? Economics answers that question. Not many companies have the resources to re-architect their systems from scratch even to take advantage of KM benefits. Cost-effective ways must be found to establish targets for architectural migration. System architecture strategies must provide a transition from the current status to a more flexible architecture that supports organizations and systems working together. These strategies must also maximize the advantages of the following:

- Increasing capabilities of large and small processors;

- Networking capabilities;

- Less complicated programming techniques;

- Understanding the benefits of sharing data (KM);

- Concentration on quality data.

The latter should be emphasized for a simple reason. Data are more permanent than processing. Data are also what tie the corporation together. Some organizations would not talk to each other at all if they did not have to exchange data. Business functionality, although basic, can usually be handled in a variety of ways, but data needed are usually stable. (After all, humans ran the business before computers.)

Improvement of the processing aspects of data processing cannot make up for the lack of historically defined quality of the data. The emphasis of quality for data can be achieved by trapping required data as close to their source as possible and leaving these data in their barest form. The long-range goal of all KM programs must be to have systems designed around the provision of quality data. There are several interim targets that can be used along the way.

An analysis of existing versus long-range target systems architecture yields the following steps for maximizing productivity of existing resources while building target system architectures:

▸ Search and destroy—eliminate redundancy of functionality and data;

▸ Surround—add flexibility to present systems;

▸ Quality data—design, plan, and implement architecture for data quality and long-term flexibility.

5.2.1 Search and destroy—eliminate redundancy

The first architectural strategy is to eliminate functional duplication and redundancy on an application by application basis. Financial and administrative systems are normally a high priority because of the need for common bookkeeping processes, payroll, and personnel systems.

In merged companies, whole systems of the current architecture are subject to elimination. However, usually, under the pressure of time requirements, systems are patched together and new feeder systems are created. Pure duplication in the systems that support operations is usually more difficult to find because the organizations coming together do not quite perform exactly the same tasks.

In some cases, a company is still determining which operations should be merged and which kept separated during IT consolidation. There usually are not a great number of whole systems that can be eliminated or much major functionality disabled, but costs can be reduced by eliminating any duplication of less than whole systems or major functions. However, this is difficult because the current architectures are usually quite inflexible and costly to modify. Therefore, it is usually determined at merge time that the largest part of the current architecture should be continued for some period of time.

This determination seemed quite appropriate at that time. However, company operations start to change. Some of the work done by separate organizational entities starts to be done by consolidated groups. KM work requires that people get data from multiple systems in the current architecture. A strategy has to be developed that can allow users to get to multiple old systems from the same terminal in order to do their work functions.

5.2.2 Defining core data or what is to be mined

The first of the new traumas facing the convert manager is the definition of corporate or "core" data. Core data in its smallest component (in the vernacular of data analysis this is usually third normal form) are those data that are essential to the functionality of the business. They are not financial report data or organizational data or not even previously defined customer data (those data with which the manager is familiar). Those data may not be the previously most used data or most redundantly stored data, although the latter is probably a good indicator. Core data cannot be defined until the company's business functions are well defined.

Defining business functions is difficult and must involve interdepartmental or corporate planners. It's too important to be left to data processing planners. Business functions are distinct from departmental goals or even business objectives. Business functions are the detail of what the business does and how it does it. Hard looks at business functions result in strange new descriptors for the work of the organization, generally under the headings of management control, operations, support, and planning. Only after these overall functions are broken down can planners really determine what data are necessary to perform the functions and determine where to find the source of highest-quality data.

The science of data analysis is becoming better defined each day, but the art of agreement as to which data belong to departments and which are core data is ill defined. The practice of charging back the costs of data processing to the user has reduced IT budgets over the years while bringing in more hardware and software, but it has also engendered a very proprietary feeling toward systems and data on the part of the users. Individual departments believe, since they paid for its conversion, processing, and storage, that they own these data. Upper management intervention is usually required to settle arguments and establish the general rules for the shared use of data. As if upper management intervention isn't traumatic enough, the reason for defining core data is to share these data. This is not always recognized by all participants, leading to psychological manifestations such as sibling rivalry or who has the biggest ego (or budget). Who pays the bill is essential to the establishment of corporate KM policy.

Arguments about the required security of data will also surface and must be resolved. As data are used for more functions of KM, especially competitive advantage, there will be more need for protection of these data from hostile eyes. The problem will be the determination of whose eyes are hostile and what harassment, in the form of password, encryption, or our right to nonaccess will be required.

5.2.3   The data engine

Once it is agreed what should be core or shared, and after the security issues have been resolved, data must go through three steps before storage, as follows:

1. The one source of the smallest component of the data must be identified. Basically this step determines from where and how basic data will enter the storage system. This step is essential in establishing the quality framework of the system. The rules for data integrity must be established here.

2. Standard identification and the catalog structure must be determined. The user must understand what these data really are and how they are identified. The use of "directories" seems to be a way to solve this problem. (See the following section.)

3. A standard output interface must be defined. The calling terminology and the access rules to data must be spelled out fully.

The preceding three steps are usually performed by technicians, but the result generates some syntax that must be understood by managers to get the full benefit of core data. Learning new language and codes has great psychological ramifications.

5.2.4   There must be directories

A directory, or more correctly a metadirectory, is a specialized repository that contains lists of system users and their access rights (for more on directories, see Chapter 8). It also functions as a kind of network white pages, giving users a simple way to locate applications, print services, and other computing resources. Some metadirectories (Microsoft's Windows 2000 Active Directory Services) add IP and network management functions to the directory. The directory also plays a role in system administration, providing IT managers a listing of all the hardware and software assets in a far-flung enterprise. Most important, a directory is a tool to integrate applications and business units that have functioned as standalone systems in the past—a great breakthrough in most organizations.

Today, directories exist in a multitude of applications ranging from a network operating system and asset management system to e-mail and database applications. The cost of implementing and administrating these disparate and often proprietary directories is great. That's why many companies are moving to implement a single, master directory, which can integrate these diverse systems. The business value of a unified directory is compelling: the elimination of redundancy and the automation of business processes across an entire enterprise.

5.2.5 Surround-increase flexibility of present systems
In addition to accessing multiple systems functionality from the same terminal to increase flexibility, KM demands the ability to distribute data from those systems so that users can add their own functionality. The Gartner Group has developed a rather complex seven-stage model depicting the evolution to client-server architecture (Figure 5.2).

Figure 5.2 is a simplified model indicating the shift from a single-purpose data processing system (in many cases that is a current corporate architecture on a mainframe) through a separation of some processing (which may include a server computer or smart terminals) leading to a

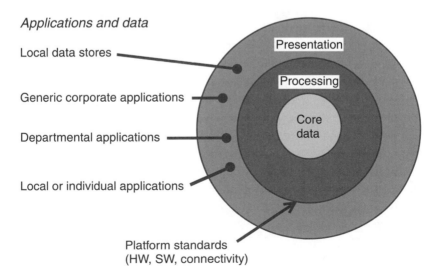

Figure 5.2   The conceptual model.

networked system with the possible use of all the processing tools with access to data that could be stored almost anywhere in the network?

Currently available computer hardware, software, and network products can be used to accomplish a partial distribution of data processing on a step-by-step basis. Legacy systems can be accessed without renetworking every terminal and without multiple log-on and log-off procedures. A server can be programmed to emulate the current terminal/mainframe interface. Data can be accessed using the current data management schema. This can be done with the same or enhanced security requirements with little additional communication time. In addition, with the use of different communication and database management software, file segments or whole files can be downloaded for different local processing.

The surround approach can be implemented with minimal complication to present mainframe processing or database software. The present application programs require modest modifications; some "add-on" programming is required to meet interface standards. Local area networking technology helps resolve communication delays. The distribution of computer and storage devices can provide resources for local development and capability for additional centrally developed systems such as electronic mail and office automation. With the use of a tightly controlled standards process for software distribution and data security, there is potential for departmental reports processing, site-oriented database administration, or other user-generated programming at each site or from a combination of sites. This is the start of KM; however, it does mean additional costs.

The great advantage to the surround approach is that it decreases the need for mainframe program modification. It leaves the current mainframe databases as they are. New user functionality can be recreated using server-based programming, which can be generated faster and cheaper than mainframe programs can be enhanced. By not having to get into mainframe languages or database management systems for every change required by users, analysts and programmers can have more time to apply their knowledge and experience to developing a long-term view of systems architecture.

5.2.6 Quality data structure

The "search" portion of search and destroy takes a detailed look at the processing and data of the current architecture. Surround uses what is learned in search and links data and processing and attempts to meet changed business needs. The long-term view should introduce the concept of a functional orientation as opposed to the traditional organizational approach to doing business (that's what reengineering is all about).

The theory is to examine what functions are required to best serve the needs of the corporation's customers and then to determine how best to accomplish those functions. A functional model of the corporation should be constructed. When the functional model is understood, data needed to support the business functions must be defined and the source described. These data must then be standardized and a corporate data directory built to ensure that these data are of the highest quality and that these data stay that way.

As discussed by Richard Y. Wang in *Communications of the ACM*, it might be necessary for corporations to manage data as they manage products. Many companies, thanks to the Japanese and Dr. Deming, are taking a total quality management approach to more of the business. This means total work force commitment, management responsibility, and a complete customer focus in attacking work processes. This kind of approach is necessary in defining core data and even more so in building the systems and procedures to keep quality data.

5.2.7 Separate the data from the processing

Close examination of data in most current system architectures indicates several potential barriers to data quality. The search to eliminate functional redundancy usually identifies significant data redundancy or apparent redundancy. There are multiple systems storing the same data (Figure 5.1) but coming from different sources. There are multiple systems storing different data from the same source. There are systems deriving and storing summarized data from detail for one business purpose and other systems deriving and storing a somewhat different summarization to be used by a different business function.

Although data editing and quality checking were stressed when individual systems were built, the combination of data that may be used for KM purposes was not preplanned or coordinated. An obvious problem with the current architecture is the cost of resources for processing and storage for the redundant data. The more serious problem, however, is the lack of confidence generated when a user confronts nonmatching data while trying to solve a customer problem. Redundant data or apparent redundancy are not quality data.

Use of poor quality data causes slow reaction to customer needs and poor customer satisfaction. Resolution of the data redundancy/quality problem is simple—separate data from the processing and build a data engine, as mentioned previously.

5.2.8　Conceptual model

Thinking about data separated from processing leads to a layered approach. This approach is only feasible through well-defined, strictly enforced standards dealing with hardware, software, and connectivity. These rules form a standard operating environment, which must be in place to allow access to shared data. A conceptual systems model depicts three layers, as follows:

1.　The core data necessary to accomplish business functions;

2.　Processing of transactions necessary to get core data into and out of databases;

3.　Presentation or other manipulation of core or local data required by the user (Figure 5.3).

5.2.9　Supporting technology

The conceptual model does not imply any specific hardware implementation, but certain inferences can be derived based on changing technology. In the current architecture, terminals connected to mainframes are used to gather, edit, and store data (Figure 5.3). Mainframe programming formats reports and rearranges data on terminal screens. Mainframes summarize and restore data. All data processing and presentation can be done with mainframe programming. With the capabilities of new technology, opportunities are available to use mainframes, servers, and personal computers (PCs) to greater advantage through networking.

To store core data in the smallest logical component, find these data, and provide all the required derivations, it will be necessary to use complex relational data structures and directories. The processing power required (even with special database machines) indicates that mainframes may be required to build and maintain large shared databases. However, the processing of those data, or the manipulation of the transactions that get these data into and out of the system, could be done with servers.

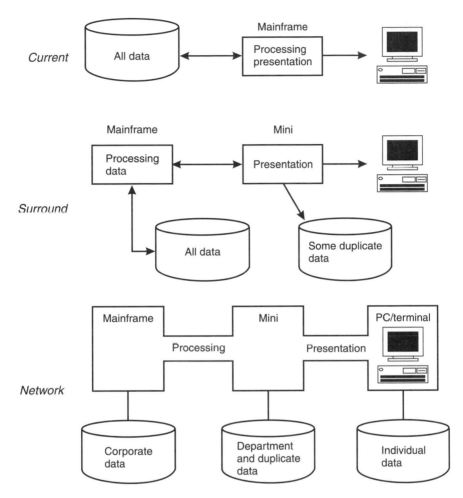

Figure 5.3 Technological architecture.

5.2.10 The "look" or the "content"?

Once consistent quality data are available, presentation—the way data look on output—can be driven closer to the user to provide flexibility. All of the formatting of these data can be done outside the mainframe, thereby reducing the load on the communications facility. (Terminal emulation mode requires that all screen format characters, as well as data, be exchanged with the mainframe. Studies indicate that by only sending data, communications requirements can be cut by orders of magnitude.) The programming could be done in a server for a group of users to analyze data in the same manner or in a networked PC if the display is for an individual.

Although this new technological approach (the processing definition of quality) is important to architectural planning, it is more important to analyze functions and data required for functions before jumping into the technology. The surround approach and the uses of new technology will produce some better efficiencies and add some flexibility at a reasonable cost (if local enhancement capabilities are very carefully accounted for), but the quality roadblock cannot be eliminated unless corporate data are standardized and made available for all processing. In the long run, a redesign of major systems around the use of quality data is required. A combination of moving to new technology while achieving quality data is ideal.

5.3   Implementing a KM strategy

The idea of redesigning major systems around quality data or anything else seems to be an anathema in these days of cutbacks. A greater problem is that data planning is difficult on a corporate scope. The whole is too big even for the best corporate and IT planners. However, planning done on an organizational basis will bring about another generation of new, improved, and faster nonquality systems. It is possible to identify clusters of data to single source and start sharing. Search will identify data that are currently being shared. Savings achieved in elimination of redundancy in destroy process can be used to pay for extra hardware needed for the surround process.

Each of these strategies refines the data sharing process until it becomes practical (either through cost justification or some less tangible value judgment) to separate certain specific data and build a data engine. It is impractical to reimplement most operational support systems at one time to make a great leap forward. The better plan is to move from the current architecture to a series of interim architectures, each becoming more quality-data oriented (Figure 5.4).

Search and destroy should be pursued not only to save money but also to identify and to start the elimination of redundant data. A logical separation can begin with implementation of the surround approach for specific functions. Most of this hardware can remain in place to transfer

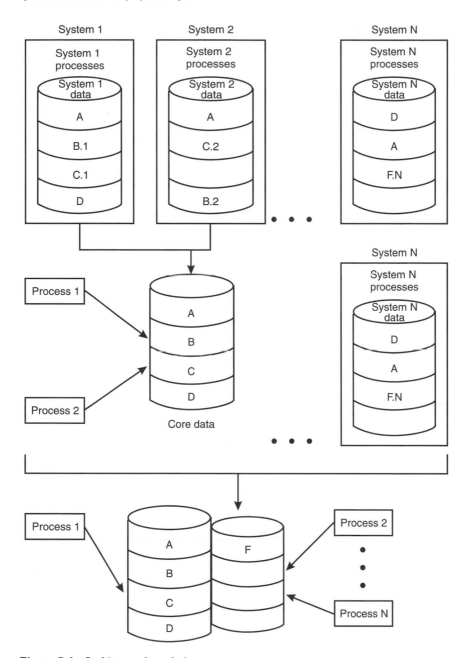

Figure 5.4 Architectural revolution.

to processors in the conceptual model. Concentration on quality data can begin by examining each new mechanization project in light of its use of standard core data.

As practical clusters of data are identified, data engines should be designed that provide the storage structure and distribution of corporate data using the presently installed mainframes. All present database systems should be examined to determine modifications needed for interim data systems and methods for converting and merging data into the next generation of engines. Over time, with new systems and high-priority modification required by present systems, the goal of quality data can be reached.

All aspects of quality are important to IT, but data quality is essential. Current systems architectures do not support economical data sharing or take advantage of new technology. Future systems will be designed around the use of quality data stored in their smallest component and available for all processing. Networking will provide the advantages of the best properties of mainframes, minicomputers, and PCs. Surround structures are an interim approach, providing continuing use of the current architecture while laying the hardware base for the transition to transaction and presentation processing of the future. A plan of migration can be developed targeting an ever increasing sharing of data until the future design can be realized.

5.3.1   KM side benefit

The technical architecture of the evolved storage structure shows the repository of core data, but it also implies that core data can be duplicated and that departmental and individual data can be defined. This means that after definition of core data there must be further definitions of the storage structure. Core data will be used for traditional corporate data processing—that is, turning these data into information for corporate reports, payroll, and so on—but data in its information (output or presentation format) will never be kept in a corporate information base. A dollar-saving aspect of getting ready for KM is that only data will be kept.

Summarizations will never be retained in the corporate database. They will just be generated on output. Customer bills will never be found in bill format in the corporate database. Storage backup will be less data intensive and cost less, but users must now address that database with the proper language to retrieve year to date or quarterly results or to create a bill status when handling customer inquiries. A hard copy of a customer bill will never be retained. Archiving, if the medium is cheap enough (microform or laser storage technology), can be on an information basis.

"What if" games will now be done outside the mainframe on departmental processors (if data must be shared) or all the way out on individual PCs. Departmental data not needed for corporate processing (i.e., team sales results, training information, bowling scores, and so on), can reside only at the departmental level. Corporate data can be duplicated and reside at the departmental level if aging information is applied by the departmental processors when these data are downloaded. (Warnings that these data were downloaded at a certain time or that data are only valid until a certain time must be applied.)

Another benefit of KM will be found as corporations assess knowledge communities (as mentioned in Chapter 12). This benefit will be moderated by the new storage requirements demanded by employees trying to keep text and multimedia records downloaded from the Internet. More sophisticated identification schemes will be needed to share these data across the organization.

5.3.2 Data quality rules

Here's one last thing about data quality. There seems to be a relationship between quality data and their use. Over time data seem to become less valuable to the corporation. Out-of-date information certainly is of little value except for historical purposes. But even user data, if not updated or refreshed, also tend to cause problems. If this is true, then, just as with one's desktop or attic, some purge or "spring cleaning" should be scheduled. Ken Orr, in *Communications of the ACM,* has addressed this problem in his list of six rules for data quality. These rules are as follows:

1. Unused data cannot remain correct for very long.

2. Data quality in an information system is a function of its use, not its collection.

3. Data quality will, ultimately, be no better than its most stringent use.

4. Data quality problems tend to become worse as the system ages.

5. The less likely some data attribute (element) is to change, the more traumatic it will be when it finally does change.

6. The laws of data quality apply equally to data and metadata (directories).

5.4 Conclusion

There are many problems with rearchitecting for KM. The changes will be significant, (read: hard to explain and hard to sell). Individual or private data and individual programs will be stored only in PCs with the tightest security precautions to avoid upward contamination. Mail and/or announcement services will originate at the PC and can still be hubbed on mainframes depending on the communications networking scheme, but any storage on mainframes will be physically separated from corporate data. Formatted data, such as expense vouchers, will be input from the PC, but only corporate required data will be passed up the line. Other data will be kept in departmental files or even locally. If it is appropriate to disburse from the departmental level, the check creation or an electronic funds transfer can take place there (hopefully speeding up the process) with only financial data going to corporate. Decentralization with centralized quality data will gain a new meaning.

The psychology of change impact of such a data and information processing hierarchy as described is traumatic. Besides the knowledge of the standard identification of data needed (new codes and language) for sharing, an understanding of the storage hierarchy must be in place. Individual managers must understand which data will be shared and where to find these data. They must also understand how to legitimately avoid the sharing of data. Auditors, as the managers, will no longer be able to pull hard copies of vouchers from departmental files. They must know how to navigate to the furthest ends of the storage structure to get all the comments added by originators. *Harvard Business Review* of March/April 1999 has a good article on the strategy of this process.

Storage pricing structures will vary greatly depending on the location of data and their utilization. New charge-back allocations will have to be developed. All this takes place after the trauma of core data definition, with all its internecine battles and, yes, even the need for top management involvement in really determining the functions of the business, has been faced.

The solutions to these problems, really introducing the concepts of KM into an organization, create a new set of promises of quality, strategic impact, and even cost savings available to potential users. In my 40 years in the business world I have seen the leaders of IT, in many companies, go from radicals demanding change to conservatives embracing and fostering the status quo. It is time for that leadership and even more important general corporate leadership to get radical again. The need to prepare users for the psychological aspects of the great opportunities has never been so important. Companies must be prepared to face the challenges and the time required to do all the interdepartmental planning work required to gain the potential advantages. These factors must be understood by all before it is appropriate to move ahead.

Selected bibliography

Publications

KMWorld, November 1998

Communications News, December 1998

Data Quality for the Information Age, Artech House, 1998

Communications of the ACM, February 1998

InformationWeek, December, 1998

Beyond Computing, May 1998, March 1999

CIO, February 1999

Network Computing, January/February 1999

Harvard Business Review, March/April 1999

Enterprise Systems Journal, May 1999

Internet Web sites

www.Datawarehousing.com

www.KMWorld.com

www.CIO.com/forums/data

www.Pmp.starnetic.com/larryg/index

www.DW-institute.com

www.Datawarehousing.org

www.Dbnet.ece.ntua.gr

www.Altaplan.com/olap

Contents

Data warehousing: the storage and access of distributed information

Caitlin M. Groom
Frank M. Groom

6.1 Introduction

Over the past 40 years the data processing industry has made large strides in providing tools and solutions for the storage of corporate information in large databases, such as IBM's IMS hierarchical storage system, and DB2, IBM's relational database storage system. This was extended to the individual through the deployment of personal computers and the ability to store personal and work information locally.

The local storage was provided with relatively large hard disk capacity and small database systems for the personal computer. This was augmented in the past 15 years by document management systems and simple groupware for the sharing of project, work effort, and product information, prominently exemplified by the Lotus Notes suite of products.

Over the past 20 years many efforts were made to create corporate decision support systems where staff information professionals attempted to collect a set of data that could be retrieved and brought to bear on a particular issue when a corporate officer needed to make an executive decision. Advances in technology and the use of technology have made a significant impact on the development of these knowledge systems. Today the storage and access of these systems, sometimes called data warehousing, has become a crucial part of the learning and business process of many corporations.

In 1937, H. G. Wells said

> Both the assembling and the distribution of knowledge in the world at present are extremely ineffective, and thinkers of the forward-looking type whose ideas we are now considering, are beginning to realize that the most hopeful line for the development of our racial intelligence lies rather in the direction of creating a new world organ for the collection, indexing, summarizing, and release of knowledge, than in any further tinkering with the highly conservative and resistant university system, local, national, and traditional in texture, which already exists. These innovators, who may be dreamers today, but who hope to become very active organizers tomorrow, project a unified, if not a centralized, world organ to 'pull the mind of the world together,' which will be not so much a rival to the universities, as a supplementary and coordinating addition to their educational activities on a planetary scale.

Wells envisioned the latest technology, microfilm, as the storage medium for his *World Encyclopedia*. But even with this great improvement over the heavy and bulky hard copy, there would still be problems. "The phrase 'Permanent World Encyclopedia' conveys the gist of these ideas. As the core of such an institution would be a world synthesis of bibliography and documentation with the indexed archives of the world. A great number of workers would be engaged perpetually in perfecting this index of human knowledge and keeping it up to date," said Wells. As Wells foresaw, the difficulty in the broad-reaching information systems of the past was that they required a set of professional workers in order to obtain information from the systems. These workers collected the information pieces, related them with each other, stored them in units, indexed them so that they could be retrieved, and then selectively located, correlated, grouped, and created position reports based upon a professional information effort. They created "knowledge" from the information.

There has been an attempt to mechanize that situation where information will be precollected into related sets about a particular entity or circumstance. These information sets will be presentable at a variety of levels, each level associated with the presumed understandable level of understanding of the user—from elementary beginning users, who wish to know a general level of information about an issue; to intermediary levels, for users who have a base of knowledge and wish to acquire a working set of information on an issue; to professional workers who need state-of-the-art knowledge about an issue, such as a doctor attempting to make a diagnosis or a surgeon preparing to operate. Popular examples of information sets that are at the leading edge include the following:

1. Remote access from rural hospitals to advanced medical centers that can receive remote x-rays and return them with the associated diagnosis of the problem and recommendations for treatment.

2. Video clips and voice instructions augmented by diagrams and text for delivery to remotely located surgeons to instruct them in rarely performed procedures.

3. Vendor-provided Web data storage of technical manuals and instructions for customer technician's use when designing or configuring equipment.

6.2 Storing information

Wells's idea of microfilm storage has been replaced with newer, easier to work with devices. Computer scientists have provided a rich set of approaches for storing and finding corporate information used in the operation of a business. Employee and payroll systems store employee work, status, pay, pension, and benefits information in a record structure-oriented system. Customer service and equipment records systems are stored in similarly structured systems.

Currently these systems employ storage systems based upon a relational algebra, with the information components for each individual or item stored in fixed-length, fixed-formatted records, and a set of such records placed together sequentially in a table. Multiple tables of such records are then grouped into table spaces, each record with an identifying key field.

An index file is then created containing the keys and a pointer identifying where in a particular disk drive the record begins, such as disk number, cylinder number, track number, sector number, and block number, and possibly item number within a given block. With these identifiers the index file contains precise pointers, which are used by an access program in retrieving a record from the database.

Older legacy systems may maintain their data as a set of segments, ordered in a logical hierarchy. Once again a beginning location is found by means of an index, but particular segments of the overall record are selectively extracted to form a partial or complete record.

As organizations were decomposed into highly decentralized and small work units, each addressing a customer, customer group, or product line, groupware systems were created to hold the work product of the unit while a particular issue, order, or project was being addressed by the work team. These systems, such as Lotus Notes, tended to store their information in flat files with no record structure. Once again an index file is created to locate each information piece. Such file systems are rather inefficient. As the number of work documents becomes large, the filing system is too primitive to operate effectively. Much disk space is wasted while retrieval time is increased.

Web servers also tend to use a flat file structure due to the unpredictability of page lengths and types of enclosed components. These systems tend to fragment their information set with page content stored in one location containing formatted hot-linking code, which dynamically links the user to another site containing the physical material that is only logically contained in the original Web page.

A major breakthrough in system construction occurred in the 1980s when information pieces were combined with the small piece of program code that typically is used to process that information piece. These units, termed objects, are stored in object databases under a variety of techniques, including maintaining the object identifier components in an index file, while the object components are placed in separate files, each deemed best for that information type. Thus, attributes might be placed in one structure, such as a relational record in a table, while a video clip or JPEG picture might be placed in a flat file due to the varying and unpredictable length of each component.

The concept of storing knowledge that is considered a more refined and more complete information set is a more complex problem. Object storage structures can be employed. However, knowledge sets tend to be rather large, final-form documents, with graphs, pictures, and diagrams, as well as tables and extensive amounts of text. These items tend to be stored in flat files as BLOBs (binary large objects) of information. Even when relational database systems are used, the knowledge sets tend to overflow into multiple tables and table spaces.

Many knowledge systems are deployed for the use of corporate customers or potential customers. Cisco, for example, places complete sets of their technical documents on a Web site to be accessed by a user browser. In these situations, the users seem to be willing to step slowly through the process of finding the required information piece even when this search can be time consuming. The convenience of acquiring the knowledge just when needed seems to offset the time required to find and then download or read the information.

It is important to recognize that individual media types, such as images, video, sound, text, and still pictures, each have their own unique size, format, and appropriate record structure for storage. Thus, specific storage structures are created for each media type and databases are dedicated to containing in an efficient manner a specific media type. The most common approach employed is to create each media type as an object that can be retrieved from its specialized database by a user employing a workstation object program. The objects can then be collected as a unit in one or a set of overlapping windows for use at the workstation. A user workstation can retrieve text, sound, and images as separate entities and as stored on a common media database.

6.3 Distributing information

As corporations become more dependent on knowledge systems, and such systems become as critical to corporate and unit success as standard information systems, the robustness of knowledge systems needs to be improved. Specialized and protected sites must be created for knowledge storage with firewalls, restricting access to only those with specified access rights.

Primary storage sites are created and one or more mirror sites are created to back up the information in case the primary site is compromised.

In that case, routers can redirect traffic to the new site in a fairly rapid fashion.

Specialized sites are created where the media differ and can be more effectively stored on a specially architected storage arrangement. Special sites are also created for extracted material, which is placed in read-only data warehouses and data marts for local use.

Occasionally information is stored originally in unique sites and then extractions are made for frequently used material. This material is placed on a composite site, which aggregates information for particular use, such as production reports, market analysis, and product and customer planning sites. Increasingly these composite sites are subsequently further decomposed into a set of nested sites arranged in an interconnected mesh structure of localized work groups, and product lines, or they are geographically decentralized but internetworked to create a virtual composite site.

6.4   Accessing information

6.4.1   Object Management Group CORBA and microsoft.com

The Object Management Group (OMG), an organization supported by most of the data processing industry (over 700 members, including Sun and Hewlett-Packard), has created a standard model for the storage of objects, applications, and services, particularly in a distributed fashion. A principal component of this CORBA architecture is the CORBA Request Broker, which acts as an agent between the servers that contain the objects, applications, and offered services, and the user. Figure 6.1 presents a common view of the CORBA Request Broker.

Some of the principal reasons for using a CORBA Request Broker are that this model and associated software not only acts as an intermediary between the user and a variety of media, applications, and services, but it is also independent of the platform on which the information resides. The servers can be personal computers, workstations, larger servers, minicomputers, or mainframes. The operating systems can vary from Windows NT, UNIX, Linix, or even IBM's mainframe MVS operating systems. Even small and portable personal data assistants and their operating systems can be supported.

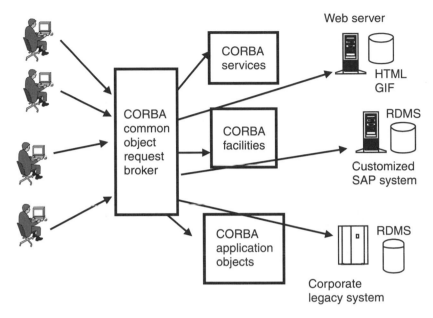

Figure 6.1 Accessing information and services by means of an object request broker.

On this wide variety of equipment, application components and objects can be written in a variety of languages, including C++, Java, Perl, and CGI.

Microsoft has offered a similar but competing approach to the OMG CORBA model. Microsoft's approach is embodied in the Component Object Model (COM), which is incorporated in all Microsoft operating systems. All vendors that develop software products for operation over Microsoft's Operating Systems, such as Windows 98, NT, and Windows 2000, support COM. Thus, COM is the foremost component in Microsoft's approach to creating a distributed environment for storing data and applications. Microsoft's overall approach to distributed operation is termed Distributed Network Architecture (DNA) and must be considered in any approach for creating a distributed version of a corporate enterprise information and/or KM system.

6.4.2 Search engines

Once a corporation has distributed information on servers throughout its operating facilities, users must be able to find where particular information and knowledge sets have been placed. We have all become familiar over the past few years with access information by means of publicly available Internet search engines, such as Yahoo!, Lycos, WebCrawler, and AltaVista.

As companies begin to move more of their corporate data out from traditional relational databases to simpler systems, browser access has become increasingly important. In order to provide their employees access to information through browser technology, such as Netscape Communicator or Internet Explorer, private internal search engines have become a required component to the user's desktop. Browser technology employed by users for the purpose of locating the Web site and file where their required information resides, and for processing a simple extraction, is generally considered a standard user requirement.

6.4.3   Client-server architectures

In the late 1980s and early 1990s, corporations began constructing their systems in a combined client-server architecture. As mentioned earlier, the idea was to separate a single program into two parts: One would be moved to the user's personal computer, and the other would remain on the server. The two-part program then operates as if it were still one. The additional enabling technology is a set of application program interfaces (API), one on the client and the other on the server, that hide the fact that a network connection is enacted when the two parts of the program need to convey information to each other.

Software and networking provider companies perceived an opportunity to assist in this process by providing an intermediary software package termed "middleware." Middleware not only hides the network connection, but in fact removes it from the user's PC and places it on a separate computer in the network, or, alternatively, leaves the network connection on the user's PC but hides the network that it accesses.

Companies then discovered that they could separate the server application component, which is paired with the user's application component, and the data that the user is seeking to retrieve or update. These data could be placed on a server that specializes only in storing and retrieving data, while the application component can be placed on a server that specializes in processing large applications. This approach is termed a three-layered client-server architecture and is portrayed in Figure 6.2.

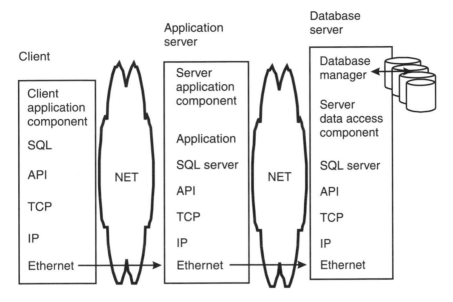

Figure 6.2   Emerging three-layer client-server model.

6.4.4   Distributed data

Finally, as organizations became decentralized and were located close to the customer served or where production facilities were located, corporate data were similarly separated and located close to the user community. These data still, for many purposes, need to be used as a complete unsegmented set. Thus, these data are only physically decentralized but remain logically in one database at a central location. These data can be accessed locally, but special precautions must be taken when these data are locally updated to protect the integrity and validity of these stored data.

However, the decentralization of corporate data added another layer of complexity to accessing information. Corporate systems tend to be created in one of the following ways:

1. Legacy mainframe systems, programmed in COBOL, with data stored in hierarchical or relational databases and accessed by means of SNA networks.

2. Client-server structured systems that have specialized APIs for the clients (termed remote procedure calls) and that store their

data in relational databases, such as those provided by Oracle and Sybase.

3. Workgroup systems, such as Lotus Notes, that have a classical document portion and a paired Web portion (the Domino addition).

4. Complete supply chain and fully integrated corporate systems such as those provided by SAP and Oracle, which likely use a relational database but tend to have their own specialized client application to operate on the user's PC for use in accessing the central system and retrieving information.

5. Web server systems, which store information in HTML format, exchange information using the hypertext transport protocol (HTTP), and may be programmed with Perl and CGI software system.

This variety of systems, as portrayed in Figure 6.3, has led to a need for combinations of browser and client software on the user's personal

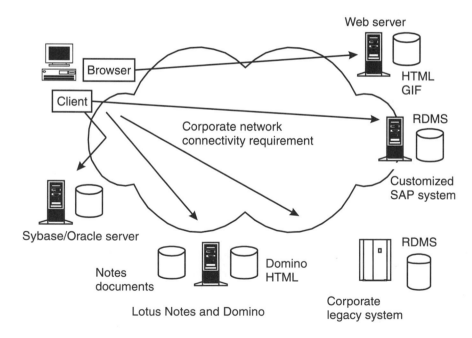

Figure 6.3 Accessing information from a heterogeneous set of system and storage types.

computer. Java programmed scripts placed on the user's PC can now be used to emulate specialized client software so that a single browser application can be employed for accessing each of these dissimilar system types.

6.4.5 Object database structures

A common approach to storing objects in a universal object database is to employ an index file in a small relational file structure. The index file contains a relational record for each object. The index record then contains a pointer in the field area for each type of information contained in the object. This allows each component to be stored in a file structure and database specialized for that record structure.

The collection of separate databases, each specialized to a particular object component—whether it be attributes and pointers, processing method software code, or picture and video files—is then treated as a composite object database. The only actual place where the object is together as a unit is in the index, where it is logically together as a set of

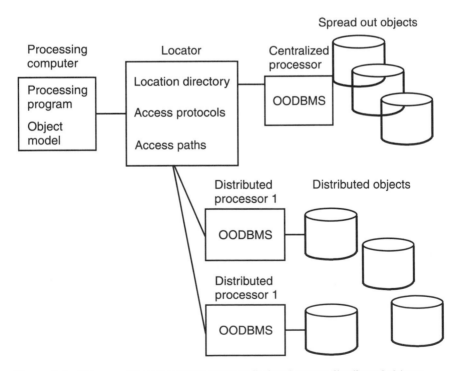

Figure 6.4 Using an object locator package to find and access distributed objects.

pointers with a common object identification used as the key to the complete object. The pointers in the index fields direct the access off to particular files for the specific components that comprise the complete object.

As objects are distributed throughout the locations of a corporation, a specific object locator system needs to be built to keep track of the location of each corporate object, the network and network protocol used to traverse the network to the specific object database location, and any specifics associated with the indexing and storage techniques employed at that specific site. Such a locator system is portrayed in Figure 6.4.

6.5   Using RAID technology for storage and protection

As information and knowledge have become so critical to the operation of a company as it operates in a moment-to-moment basis, merely backing up storage disks on a regular basis may lose precious moments of information use that can be damaging to the corporation. RAID (redundant array of independent disks) technology is frequently deployed to address information security as well as speed of access at a strikingly reduced cost. By using RAID disks each record is striped across a set of disks. This approach is especially useful for large records, which contain multimedia components such as pictures and sound, as well as text and data. Retrieval time is reduced, since each disk contains only a portion of each record. Retrieval is a parallel process. For example, if the records are striped across five disks (each disk containing one-fifth of the record), retrieval time proceeds in parallel and is reduced by four-fifths the usual time. More advanced RAID levels provide for a parallel set of disks (in our example ten disks instead of five). The second set of disks would have a duplicate copy of the initial record striping and can be used if the original set is damaged in some fashion.

Still other approaches, such as RAID 4 and 5, use a separate parity disk in place of the duplicate set of disks to provide data recovery, while RAID 6 duplicates the primary parity disk on a second parity disk. Still further RAID approaches are currently being implemented including RAID 7, 10, 0+1, and RAID 53, each providing still another variation on the striping, mirroring, and parity recovery processes. Such storage technology offers many opportunities for distributed databases, Web databases, and data warehousing, where the volume of information to be stored and the criticality of it to the user community requires speed to access, low cost, and a higher level of reliability and recovery than offered by standard disk storage approaches.

6.6   The data warehouse for storing information

By the end of 2001, it is estimated that $5 billion will flow into the data warehousing arena. One midwestern financial institution has data on 3.3 million households. Many companies have spread their facilities across a country, continent, or have become a global operation. They frequently have decided, for operational purposes, to extract selected data from the corporate on-line transaction processing systems that are primarily mainframe and distributed client-server systems providing daily support to the operations of the business.

The extracted information is then downloaded to a transforming system, which selects particular information pieces and groups them and formats them for particular user access. Most of the information is then further downloaded to a central corporate data warehouse system, which maintains corporate information as read-only sets. Further, selected information components are then segmented off from the warehouse and downloaded to local storage close to individual work centers for quick and repeated access and use as part of daily work activity.

The mainframe corporate transaction systems provide the primary storage for corporate information. This information, as well as the systems that update, maintain, and provide information for the primary business processes of the enterprise, is protected with limited access, passwords, and specialized network connections. The stored information is a formal record kept by the company of all corporate transactions. These mainframe and client-server systems provide quick second or subsecond response to dedicated entry and processing support personnel.

Data that have been moved to the data warehouse are combined into structures for user access for strategy, marketing, and planning purposes. Access to this large cluster of information frequently takes minutes for response from the system. The expectation is that users have the time to wait for the search mechanisms to explore those data and collect sets of data to match the parameters of the user request. Warehouse data are stored by type rather than by the application that originally maintained it. Thus, data are stored in only one part of the warehouse database, even though these data are used in many different combinations with many other data components for specialized user requirements.

Data in the warehouse are coupled with a time stamp associated with the time at which these data were entered in the primary system or data warehouse. Daily new versions of the same type of information are added, each with its own unique time stamp. Thus, data are really stored as a series of snapshots of a particular event, each representing a period of time.

Data in the warehouse can be dynamically combined to produce forecasts, strategies, customer profiles, and unit plans. Since only the corporate source in the mainframe systems undergoes the full treatment to satisfy legal and government requirements, the warehouse data are only meant to be used for extraction and manipulation. These data are thus read-only data and should not be updated or deleted by a user action.

With corporate units now distributed around the globe, it is frequently more appropriate for some units to further download a subset of the data warehouse's stored information set. Only the information appropriate to a market subset, a geographical area, or a product set might be placed close to the work unit for quick and continual access in the daily process of business. The flow of information from the source mainframe systems to the warehouse and local data marts is portrayed in Figure 6.5.

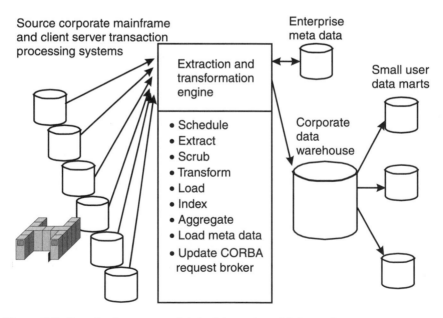

Figure 6.5 Transferring process data to data marts and data warehouses.

6.7 Using the Web as a warehouse

The World Wide Web is not a network in a traditional sense. The Web actually is a set of information servers that is attached to the Internet but is not directly a part of the Internet. While at CERN in Switzerland, Tim Berners-Lee introduced the combination of hypertext mark-up language, hypertext transport protocol, and the concept of creating virtual documents out of material placed on databases at a variety of Web sites.

As envisioned by Berners-Lee, the Web is a way to link documents so that the components of a document can be placed in many locations throughout the world on Web-enabled servers attached to the Internet. These document components are "marked up" with indicators at the beginning and end of each line. Some of the lines of a document contain links to content instead of containing the actual content itself. This allows for the virtual inclusion of pictures, graphs, more detailed documents, references, and diagrams in a document.

It is a very effective way to include multimedia components in the original document, such as video clips, by a linking reference without the clumsy inclusion of dissimilar material in a stored text document. When such a hypertext marked-up document is downloaded from an Internet attached server to a requesting user's browser, the user may click on the link in the document, which results in another request over the Internet to the new location and its additional stored component.

A set of these "hot links" may be placed throughout an original base document, or each subsequently linked document can have its own links to further sites. Figure 6.6 portrays access to an original document that is further linked to two other documents in other sites that are also attached to the Internet. Thus, a complete document can be dispersed across a number of sites, as a virtual document, allowing the user to retrieve component parts at the user's discretion. So Figure 6.6. portrays a user employing a browser to request information from one site with hot links to two others, thus providing the retrieval of a virtual document stored at three sites.

Among many Web sites that provide information, a number of organizations provide complete knowledge sets, which define the current state of understanding in a particular area. One of the more interesting examples of this is the site at Cambridge University, which provides a rather complete knowledge base of current cosmological thinking about the creation and on-going expansion of the universe. This site contains a

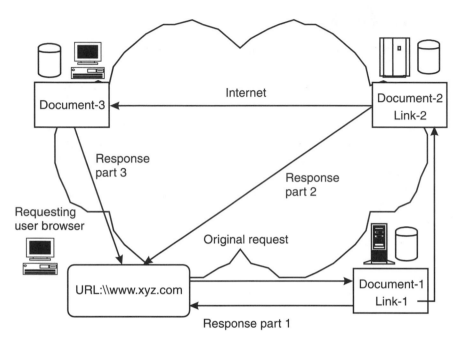

Figure 6.6   The storage of information in linked Web databases.

core set of information about the Big Bang and the subsequent steps in the cosmological operation, as well as links to movies that actively portray the process as it unfolds.

6.8   Conclusion

Again, as H. G. Wells foresaw, globally stored and presented information presents particular cultural and language problems for user and international researchers searching for appropriate information. Nothing is more irritating than finding exactly the knowledge set that one requires only to find that it is written in French, German, or a language other than one's own. Fortunately, many search engines, such as AltaVista, are creating translator routines, which can be employed as a beginning approach to understanding the material.

Other software is being developed with particular technical and business dictionaries to provide a more complete translation of the knowledge set. This process appears to hold out great hope for the Americas and Western European countries. However, more than half the world—the emerging and frequently most attractive portion due to its large potential markets, trained work forces, and low wage rates—is not western-oriented with our common romance languages.

Countries and regions of the globe also are dissimilar in their concepts of time, what is important in life, and religious beliefs. These dissimilarities can lead to entirely different processes of working with information. In the United States and Western Europe we have become acclimated, since Isaac Newton, to perceiving time as a constant vector with determined unvarying intervals. This concept has led to the process of thinking in a cause-and-effect approach to problems and issues, as well as thinking in a linear fashion about working through a problem in successive steps until we reach a conclusion. Other cultures may view the same issues as societal, religious, or territorial. Thus, documents that are created under one perspective may be unusable in another, may be misused, or may in fact be offensive to another culture.

Businesses that are global in their operation and customer base must take contextual concepts in consideration when they are constructing systems that store fully formed knowledge sets. Standard database systems store their information in fields and records that are less susceptible to interpretation. Moreover, they tend to be numerical and attribute oriented, thus lessening the opportunity for added interpretation and misinterpretation.

Wells went on to say

> Few people as yet, outside the world of expert librarians, and museum curators and so forth, know how manageable well-ordered facts can be made, however multitudinous, and how swiftly and completely even the rarest visions and the most recondite matters can be recalled, once they have been put in place in a well-ordered scheme of reference and reproduction. There is no practical obstacle whatever now to the creation of an efficient index to all human knowledge, ideas, and achievements, to the creation, that is, of a complete planetary memory for all mankind. And not simply an index; the direct reproduction of the thing itself can be summoned to any properly prepared spot. This in itself is a fact of tremendous significance. It foreshadows a real intellectual unification of our race. The whole human memory can be, and probably in a short time will be, made accessible to every individual.

His timing was off, but he may have been thinking in the right direction.

Selected bibliography

Alvarez, G. A., W. A. Burkhard, and F. Cristian. "Tolerating Multiple Failures in RAID Architectures with Optimal Storage and Uniform Declustering." In *Proceedings of the Twenty-fourth Annual ACM/IEEE International Symposium on Computer Architecture*.

Balou, Donald. "Enhancing Data Quality in Data Warehouse Environments." *ACM* (January 1999).

Bank, David. "Engineer Group Is Backing New Protocol to Handle Large Blocks of Data on Web." *Wall Street Journal* (January 25, 2000).

Gains, Brian, and Mildred Shaw. "Embedding Formal Knowledge Models in Active Documents." *ACM* (January 1999).

Jong, Kevin, "Evolutionary Computation for Discovery." *Beyond Computing* (July/August 1999): *ACM*, (November 1999).

Purao, Sandeep, Hemant Jain, and Derek Nazareth. "Effective Distribution of Object-Oriented Applications." *ACM* (August 1998).

Rob, Peter, and Carlos Coronel. Database Systems: Design, Implementation, and Management. 4th ed. Course technology, Thompson Learning, 1999.

Schmidt, Douglas. "Evaluating Architectures in Multithreaded Object Request Brokers." *ACM* (October 1998).

Selvia, John. "Kanji Characters." http://www.dnaco.net/%7Eivanjs/kanji21_30.html.

Siegal, Jon. "OMG Overview: CORBA and the OMA in Enterprise Computing." *ACM* (October 1998).

Singh, Narinder. "Unifying Heterogeneous Information Models." *ACM* (May 1998).

Terplan, Kornel. *Web-Based Systems and Network Management*. Boca Raton, FL: CRC Press, 1999.

Valdez-Perez. "Discovery Tolls for Science Applications." *ACM* (November 1999).

Vinoski, Steve. "CORBA: Integrating Diverse Applications within Distributed Heterogeneous Environments." *IEEE Communications* (February 1997).

www.sunworld.com

Contents

An integrated development model for KM

Feng Kwei Wang
Josh Plaskoff

7.1 Introduction

Over the past few years, KM has leaped to prominence in business and computer journals and has reached the status of "top priority" in many major companies' business strategies. As companies recognize that a critical corporate asset is tied up in intellectual capital and embedded in the people, processes, and products of the organization, knowledge, like money, becomes something that must be managed to optimize return on investment.

Accompanying this emergence, though, is also a great deal of confusion about what KM is. Indeed, there is little agreement about what knowledge is. Many have jumped on the KM bandwagon without tackling these difficult definitional questions and, as a result, have clothed data management, information management, or just plain database application development in the cloak of KM. This hastiness has led to failed or, at best, suboptimized initiatives. Without developing a holistic model of KM, practitioners can never attain a systematic approach that addresses KM's many facets.

The purpose of this chapter is twofold. After defining some terms—namely, the commodity of interest (knowledge) and the process applied to it (KM)—we will present an integrated development model for KM: one that addresses not only its technological but also its organizational and process aspects. Then, we will describe how this model played out in the creation of a system at Eli Lilly and Company, the original context of its creation. By reading this chapter, you will gain a much more holistic perspective of KM and be able to prepare for design and implementation of KM initiatives.

7.2 Defining the problem

Before we can dive into a formulation of KM, it is first critical that we define the commodity with which we are dealing. In the financial world, determining what needs to be managed is much easier because those assets are tangible. What we are dealing with here, however, is very intangible, fuzzy, and poorly defined. As a result, many efforts shy away from initially defining knowledge and make the assumption that everyone already knows what knowledge is, which is one of the biggest errors made on KM projects [1].

In epistemology, the standard definition for knowledge is "justified true belief." While this is good for philosophers, it does little to help clarify things for the business world. We prefer to view knowledge as information infused with insight and experience. Knowledge and information, and for that matter data, are not synonymous. Data have no context or meaning by themselves. Information is data that have meaning and context.

Knowledge is information with personal or organizational insight and experience that add value to the person or organization as a result of productivity gains and innovation. Information does not become knowledge in a vacuum. Knowledge is embedded in and generated through information transforming processes. Through processing, new knowledge is created, reshaped, reused, and transferred to other people, processes, and products. The primary agent of these operations is people.

This people-centered perspective of knowledge is critical as we begin to address KM.

7.2.1 What is KM?

Now that we know what knowledge is, what is KM? Knowledge management is a capability built into the business processes that enables the company to apply and add to what it collectively knows and identify what it doesn't know. It enables faster and better decision making, problem solving, and work operations to increase productivity and innovation.

KM can involve two different types of strategies: codification and personalization [2]. Codification is the strategy that captures knowledge for reuse by another entity in the company. Personalization is the strategy that connects people to collaboratively generate new solutions. One establishes the people-to-document connection, the other the people-to-people connection. These two strategies can be realized through assessing and augmenting the capabilities of an organization and its people in learning, sharing, and managing information to add personal or organizational value.

Building the capability for KM requires a holistic focus on several different elements. Technology is one of the elements. But capability also requires a focus on people, on processes, and on the organizations that support them. The remainder of this section will explain these elements of KM and develop a framework around them.

7.2.2 Framework for a KM capability

KM is more than a technological solution that gives people access to better and more relevant information. It represents, in its best use, a fundamental shift in how people relate to their work and to one another in a business environment and has the capacity to promote extraordinary collaboration and communication among and between geographically decentralized and intellectually individualized business units. It can be a bridge that allows independently operating business units to work together by sharing processes, skills, systems, and learning to support a common strategy.

To be effective, KM and business processes must mesh, and the design of the KM architecture must reflect the mindset of the workers who operate within those business processes. Thus, KM is a capability inherent in the organization and, as such, comprises the four elements

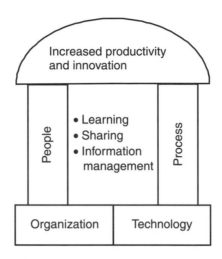

Figure 7.1 KM framework.

mentioned previously: organization, people, process, and technology (OPPT).

Using a building as an analogy (see Figure 7.1), we view organization and technology as the foundation; people and process as the pillars that maintain the structure; and learning, information sharing, and information management that supports the value-added process of transforming

Table 7.1
Variables of a KM Project

| | Change Capabilities | | Design Capabilities | |
	Organization	People	Process	Technology
Key Variables	▸ Culture	▸ Needs	▸ Task flow	▸ Functionality
	▸ Structure	▸ Expectations	▸ Variances	▸ Usability
	▸ HR policy	▸ Skills	▸ Boundaries	▸ Reliability
	▸ Social net-work	▸ Knowledge	▸ Priority	▸ Acceptability
	▸ Reinforce-ment			

information to knowledge as the inherent functionality of the building. In this regard, a KM system is comprised of knowledge workers using KM technology or tools to perform knowledge tasks in a knowledge organization with the goal of increasing organizational and individual productivity and innovation. These four OPPT constituents must function cohesively to reap the full benefits of a KM system.

In light of this, a KM project has to focus on both design (process and technology) and change (people and organization) capabilities simultaneously. This adds to the complexity of the project. To achieve these goals, a project team should study the variables of the OPPT components that support information-knowledge transforming processes identified in Table 7.1.

The outcomes of the study are a list of enablers and barriers in each OPPT constituent. An enabler is a favorable factor, which supports the project or implementation of possible solutions. A barrier is an unfavorable factor, which hinders the performances of the target audience in learning, sharing, and information management. By going through the cycle of removing barriers and leveraging enablers, the project team is able to generate KM solutions. These solutions should center around project goals. Also, in view of the required resources and available resources, these solutions should be prioritized based on their impacts, efforts, and time frames (see Figure 7.2).

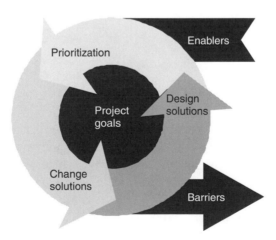

Figure 7.2 The KM project.

7.3   Solution: integrated KM development model

In the previous sections, we covered our definition of KM and some strategic foundations and models on which we based our project. In this section, we will present our tactical approach to implementing these models. We outline each phase's overall process and then provide some specific details about carrying out that process.

7.3.1   Background

From 1997 to 1999, a team of Lilly employees and external consultants began the process of creating a complete KM system in a research organization within Lilly Research Laboratories based on the framework presented previously. Dubbed the Scientists' Professional Innovation Network (SPIN), the project was divided into phases, each holistically addressing the four framework elements (organization, people, process, and technology) with an eye toward implementing the complete conversion cycle of knowledge creation.

7.3.2   Overall process

The SPIN project followed a standard five-phase process of the systems development life cycle (SDLC), as follows:

1.   Assessment;

2.   Requirements;

3.   Design;

4.   Development;

5.   Implementation.

One major difference between our SDLC (see Figure 7.3) and other SDLCs is that we believe technology innovation and organizational change coevolve. Technology solutions have to incorporate change solutions and vice versa. We stated earlier that people are the primary agent of any knowledge process. KM represents a major shift in how people relate to their work and to each other.

These changes are more than incidental; they are a fundamental dimension of a successful KM project. This means that a successful project must include a deliberate and well-planned process for helping

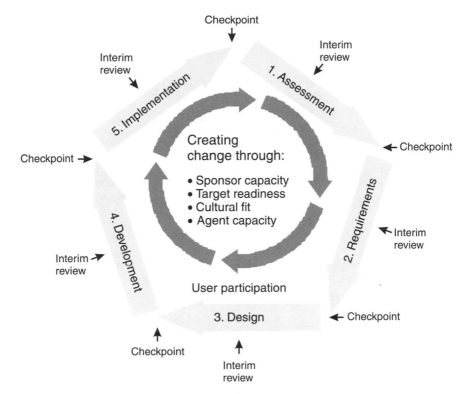

Figure 7.3 The SDLC process.

the target group change. A number of change methodologies are currently on the market. Eli Lilly and Company adopted a particular change methodology that integrates sponsorship, agency, readiness, and reward systems. This methodology served as the change framework for this project. Each phase of the SDLC process also contained checkpoints and reviews with key sponsors and participants to ensure that the solution design and change programs were proceeding as planned.

Detail about each phase, along with its focus and key deliverables, is described in Table 7.2. At the time of the writing of this chapter, only the first two phases have been completed. So this chapter will focus on the framework for "preparing" for a KM project and the lessons learned in doing that preparation. It should be noted that we separate roject initiation from assessment since this project was a new initiative at Lilly. Enormous efforts were put into the project initiation to raise KM awareness, to gain management buy-in, and to educate stakeholders. Many successful stories and lessons learned came out of this phase. They deserve a special section in this chapter.

Table 7.2
Detailed Phase Descriptions

Phase	Focus	Outcomes
Initiation		
Scan for problems or opportunities Identify initial target audience and content Conceptualize system design Develop system prototype Determine preliminary project resources	▶ Finding an appropriate project ▶ Educating stakeholders ▶ Selling the concept ▶ Assembling the project team	▶ Mission statement for the project ▶ Business case for action ▶ List of barriers to successful completion ▶ Prototype for the project ▶ Preliminary list of project resources
Assessment		
Identify issues Filter and prioritize issues Conduct root cause analysis Analyze results Present findings to stakeholders	▶ Understanding context around project ▶ Building support of target population ▶ Defining critical issues and causes	▶ Description of target organization ▶ Profile of target audience ▶ Detailed description of the organization's work ▶ List of barriers and enablers for project
Requirements		
Determine solutions Define system scope Define resources scope Secure approval for project	▶ Determining specific solutions ▶ Determining product design requirements ▶ Determining project resources ▶ Gaining support for implementation	▶ Definition of a complete solution package ▶ List of product design requirements ▶ Realistic estimate of all project costs ▶ Approval to move ahead
Design/Development	Future development	
Implementation	Future development	
Evaluation	Future development	

7.3.2.1 Phase 1: project initiation process

Overview The concept of KM is not yet part of the accepted processes and culture in many organizations, Lilly included. Therefore, the first stage of the project focused on educating others about the KM concept and selling them on its benefits. Interest was generated through educational sessions, benchmarking presentations, and brainstorming sessions with business area representatives.

This also helped to identify the specific target area—namely, the combinatorial chemistry area within the research organization. Once this area was determined, the focus shifted to gaining sponsorship from leadership at all levels by helping them conceptualize the end state through a prototype. This phase was critical to the success of the project because it established relationships between the project team and the business area; created a unified philosophy, mission, and vision for the project; and created tools that helped to sell the project to the organization.

The steps of the project initiation process are outlined in Table 7.3. Tools developed and methods used are included for each step.

Table 7.3
Project Initiation Process

Phase 1: Project Initiation	
Process Steps	**Tools and Methods**
1. Scanning the organization for problems or opportunities	‣ Networking, personal relationships ‣ Document review
2. Identifying initial target audience and content	‣ Discussions, meetings ‣ Readiness assessment
3. Conceptualizing system design	‣ Business case ‣ Project mission statement ‣ Visual project plan ‣ Change plan
4. Developing a prototype ‣ Involved users ‣ Communicated with stakeholders ‣ Revised as necessary	‣ Rapid collaborative prototyping ‣ Discussions, management meetings ‣ Communication plan
5. Determining preliminary project resources	‣ Role map

Project initiation process detail   Early meetings with senior leadership in the chemistry area sparked some interest in the project. They were interested in using the SPIN concept to help eliminate tedious administrative tasks for chemists and to help new chemists contribute to the company faster. Leadership indicated that the combinatorial chemistry group seemed to be a fruitful area. This group was responsible for developing a new chemistry methodology and diffusing it to the chemistry community at large to help expedite development of potential molecules.

It is a small and manageable group of about 15 people, all based in Indianapolis and located in the same general vicinity. An interested subject matter expert in the target population was identified, a team member who proved to be instrumental in pushing the project forward.

From project concept to prototype   Before moving forward the team needed a name for the project. It decided to create an acronym for the project that had some significance to chemists, the target audience. The name chosen was SPIN. This name was chosen for a few reasons. First, it emphasized the importance of networking in the model. Second, the acronym created was SPIN, a term referring to a characteristic of electrons in both chemistry and physics. Third, it used the word innovation, a keyword in the business strategy.

Though conversations had helped to develop the SPIN concept, it was still too fuzzy for decision makers who would be providing the funding for the project. These leaders needed something they could visualize and stand behind. A prototype proved an invaluable tool. The purpose of the prototype was as follows:

- To provide a visual and conceptual example for a sponsor who would provide funding;

- To serve as a concrete way of organizing and expanding the initial concept;

- To facilitate buy-in among the target population by enlisting their participation and helping them visualize the possibilities.

Throughout the creation of the prototype, the project team reinforced the idea with both sponsors and the target population that although the prototype was technology based, the larger SPIN project would use technology to support work processes, organizational change, new roles, and cultural change. This would be addressed after buy-in was secured from the sponsor.

The approach taken in the creation of the prototype was to develop a system that provided breadth of function as opposed to depth. It was designed to show all of the functionality that a system such as this could house, including on-line learning environments, video, multiple reference sources, automation, and discussion.

The team worked closely with two chemists to develop the system. In the end, the prototype contained both learning and reference elements, as follows:

- On-line interactive learning environment for combinatorial chemistry[1]:

  - An assessment area;

  - Case studies and a collaborative area for solving them;

  - A shared project area;

  - A seminar room for discussions.

- Reference elements:

  - Significant projects developed during the interactive learning sessions;

  - A customizable tool area with access to databases on the network;

  - A bibliography based on Endnotes, a program used by the chemists;

  - Web links;

  - Equipment demos;

  - Experimentals (descriptions and chemical representations of key reactions);

  - Personnel descriptions;

  - War stories.

---

1. Instruction on basic concepts in combinatorial chemistry is based on a stand up course developed by combinatorial chemists.

Much of the content for the prototype existed somewhere in the department, although it was spread out and not systematized. The centerpiece for the system was the on-line learning environment for combinatorial chemistry. At the time, several of the lead chemists were teaching a lecture and lab course in combinatorial chemistry that they and other chemists had developed. The chemistry organization had identified this course as a high priority for all chemists. The prototype showed how this same course could be taught to a global audience electronically. The course materials were revised and converted to an electronic format suitable for the Lotus Notes platform. Molecular structures were converted to IsisDraw, a package used by chemists for drawing and searching on molecular structures.

In addition, databases existed on the network, but chemists did not have easy access. One chemist had collected an extensive bibliography and another had collected Web links. Personnel files existed on the Web, and experimentals were codified as part of a previous knowledge transfer project.

The final prototype showcased broad functionality, as follows:

- Links between documents (from the learning system to the reference materials);

- Search;

- Links between people and documents;

- Tracking document access;

- Linking to existing databases;

- Web access;

- Bookmarking;

- Customizable tool desktops;

- Multiple functional desktops;

- Collaborative workspaces;

- Desktop video.

While the project team was creating the prototype, they attended one of the training programs to videotape it for content and to poll the chemists to see whether a solution such as this would be a better solution than sitting in a course. The results showed that use of a system such as SPIN would be welcomed.

Creating a mission or vision While the prototype served as a strong tool for visualizing the technology of the project, it did not help in creating a business case or holistic vision for the project. The team with the chemists brainstormed a mission and vision statement that would be compelling but would also speak in the language of the chemists.

After much wrestling a mission statement was created: "SPIN is an integrated solution to increase productivity and innovation among chemists through sharing expertise and providing better access to combinatorial chemistry resources. SPIN is not just a computer solution but also addresses the processes and culture of the chemist's work environment." The last sentence was critical, since it again emphasized the importance of integrating technology, people, processes, and organization. The mission statement was laminated in credit card format and each team member carried it to deliver a consistent message.

Recruiting support With the prototype completed, the organization, people, and process components needed to be wed to the technology. To generate interest both in the chemistry community and throughout the company, the SPIN project team gave many presentations about the prototype. Most of these presentations were one on one, targeted particularly at people who could have an impact on the chemistry community— intelligence center, organizational effectiveness, HR line in the chemistry organizations, and IT. These presentations also served as a recruitment device for creating other teams in the future.

Several meetings were scheduled with the president of the target organization. The first conversations involved describing the concept of the prototype and the business case and how it linked into what the chemists were currently teaching in the combinatorial chemistry course. Future conversations expanded to discuss the cultural and process changes needed in the organization to create more sharing and learning among the chemists.

Discussions and interest grew over a period of several months and in July 1998 the president sanctioned the SPIN project. One of the chemists who had been involved from the outset and was instrumental in creating the prototype was assigned to the project and the president took the responsibility of sponsorship.

Organic chemists are naturally visual people who are successful because they can visualize three-dimensional chemical structures. To aid these chemists in visualizing the project as a whole, a visual project plan was created. Based on a car-racing theme, a wall chart showed each of the deliverables and key activities in a pictorial motif. The Steering Committee was the pit crew, the cars displayed were the sponsoring organizations, and the chemists were the drivers. The plan was used to further help the chemists and their management picture the entire process of building the SPIN system.

7.3.2.2   Phase 2: assessment

Overview   Once the project received the go ahead, the next step was a thorough assessment of the current state of the environment. This assessment used the OPPT framework. It examined what and how the target audience learns, shares, and manages information and knowledge within its particular organizational context and sought to uncover the critical issues that hinder specific predetermined performance issues of the target audience. By identifying the critical performance issues and then identifying the barriers and enablers of these issues, the project team was able to devise a solution plan to improve performance.

The steps of the Assessment phase are outlined in Table 7.4.

Assessment process detail   During the assessment phase, the change function of the project was formally added to the team, which partnered an internal team member with a consultant to facilitate knowledge transfer about the process from the outside to the inside. The change team began to work on the change tasks necessary for success on the project: sponsorship, strengthening relationships, business cases, communication, and readiness.

SPIN's business case was crafted very early in the process and approved by the steering committee in initial discussions. The business case linked the change to the overall business strategy and addressed the questions of both why this change was important to the target audience and the negative consequences that might occur if the change did not happen. The business case was communicated frequently. This document became known as the "placemat," since it was put on a laminated card the size of a placemat.

The change approach to use for SPIN was to enlist high cooperation and collaboration from all parties. This was generally successful and sup-

Table 7.4

Assessment Process

Phase 2: Assessment	
Process Steps	**Tools and Methods**

1. Identify issues
  ▶ Possible issues
  ▶ Those in scope, those out of scope
	▶ Focus groups
	▶ Issues inventory

2. Filter and prioritize issues
  ▶ Determine critical issues
  ▶ Report to sponsor
	▶ Survey
	▶ Issues prioritization

3. Conduct root cause analysis	▶ Interviews ▶ Field observation ▶ Focus groups

4. Analyze results
  ▶ Synthesize data
  ▶ Propose critical issues
  ▶ Determine enablers and barriers
	▶ Group discussion
	▶ Content analysis
	▶ Descriptive statistical analysis

5. Present findings to stakeholders	▶ Management meetings

ported by the level of involvement of people in designing the project and in the attempt, through focus groups, interviews, and surveys, to ask for their input and understand the environment in which they worked.

Given the highly individualistic nature of the population the SPIN team was addressing and the goal of promoting greater sharing, learning, and collaboration as a result of the project, it was clear that the team had to impact compensation in a meaningful way to promote desired behavior. To that end, line HR was enlisted to determine the flexibility of compensation systems, inclusion of desired behaviors into individual key result areas (KRAs), and reinforcement of desired behavior by management.

As part of the overall implementation, a communication plan was drafted that articulated what messages needed to be delivered by whom, to whom, by when, and by what vehicles.

The project team   Work on the project began with the recruitment of a cross-functional team, a cross-functional steering committee, and a project plan.

The project team was recruited to achieve the maximum interaction of individual skills and political influence. Team members were recruited internally from IT, LRL training, chemistry, the intelligence center, and organizational effectiveness, as well as externally from consulting companies. This ensured that the team had adequate cross-functional representation, which allowed them to look at the many sides of issues that needed to be addressed.

The project team members comprised both a design team and a change team. Each of these specialized teams included both Lilly staff and external consultants. Because of the pairing of internal staff and external consultant, each team could operate more effectively depending on the organizational situation. Consultants often are able to ask challenging questions that internal employees cannot ask. They can also lend credibility, which sometimes is difficult for internal employees. At the same time, internal employees can sometimes negotiate some of the political blocks and barriers that a consultant would not have leverage to overcome.

In addition, the project coordinator role was added to manage the knowledge of the team. To handle the large amount of information that needed to be transferred and shared, the group set up the Lotus Notes application to collect the documentation, knowledge, and deliverables for sharing both within and outside the team.

Each subteam was given autonomy, but at the same time was required to communicate decisions and link into the other team's actions. Weekly team meetings facilitated the communication. Many decisions were made at these meetings so that all aspects of the challenge could be addressed.

A steering committee was created with same cross-functional focus. Besides the sponsoring organization, the committee included representatives from the area training function, global training function, a sister chemistry organization, the line HR organization, and the information technology organization.

Team principles   The team generated a charter, which had a number of operating principles including the following:

- ▸ The target population, the chemists, would feel that they were designing the system and that the team was facilitating the process.

- ▸ The project team made every attempt to communicate in the language of the target population.

▸ The project was a partnership between all organizations.

▸ Project communication was critical. The team was open with its findings, its knowledge, and its tools.

▸ The change and design processes were interwoven as a single project.

▸ It was critical to make sure that chemists felt that they were heard and appreciated. They were given the results of any activities and appropriately thanked by management.

▸ All members of the team had an equal say in the project.

▸ Nothing was delivered without having the appropriate maintenance and support mechanisms in place.

▸ The project was phased—a technique that "portioned out" the investment in the project and allowed close scrutiny of project feasibility at each stage.

▸ Formal celebrations accompanied the completion of major tasks and phases.

▸ The team took risks throughout the project and documented both successes and failures.

▸ Intangible and tangible deliverables were considered important.

Data collection The SPIN project team used the following data collection methods:

▸ Focus groups;

▸ Electronic survey;

▸ Interviews.

The assessment was conducted over a two-month period.

Focus groups A focus group was conducted with chemists, experienced and new, medicinal and combinatorial, to determine the issues facing chemists concerning learning, sharing, and information management. The focus of the session was to uncover as many issues as possible, whether they were applicable to SPIN or not. At the end of the project, the same group of chemists was again brought together to validate the analysis.

Electronic survey in Lotus Notes   A Lotus Notes survey was then developed based on the critical issues that were collected from the focus groups. Also included were questions concerning technology preferences and use. The survey was distributed to the entire population and peripheral chemistry organizations. The response to the survey, which represented 100% of the population, prioritized the issues. An analysis of the results both by seniority of the chemists and their organization was created.

The Lotus Notes electronic survey mechanism developed by the team proved to be very effective for easy and quick responses. Within two hours, one-third of the respondents responded, and within 24 hours, two-thirds of the surveys were returned. All the surveys were collected within one week. The survey was sent as an e-mail message to respondents with a cover letter from the project sponsor. A click on the "Finish the Survey" button at the bottom of the cover letter replaced the content with the survey instructions and questions.

On finishing the survey, the respondents clicked the "Submit" button on the top or at the end of the survey to send back the survey via e-mail. Confidentiality was maintained by erasing the "sent by" field on the return e-mail. Respondents were also given the opportunity to fax responses back, which only a few did.

Interviews   Key issues revealed by the survey were compiled into a series of interview guides. The purpose of the interviews was to uncover root causes behind the issues. Interviews were held with chemists from various organizations, HR line, management, and IT. Five teams of two people (a primary interviewer and secondary interviewer) were created to perform the interviews.

An interview guide and note-taking form were created before every interview (since some of the interviewees received specialized questions pertaining to their area) and those forms were mailed to the interviewer and secondary interviewer the day before the interview. Interviews were 1½ hours long and were kept strictly confidential. Some were taped and transcribed.

In addition to interviews, some team members worked with chemists in the lab to observe their daily tasks and uncover barriers to learning, sharing, and information management.

Analysis   A large amount of data was collected for analysis: survey data, interview results, observations in the lab, and focus group feedback. To analyze these data, all responses and issues were collected and then iteratively grouped and edited until major themes were uncovered. Responses that did not have any corroboration from others were considered to be individual issues and were eliminated, as were issues and causes that were not part of the scope of the project.

The groupings were then assigned to categories (organization, people, process, and technology) and classified as a barrier or enabler. These groupings were conducted as a team exercise. These issues and causes were then prioritized, again as a team. What resulted was a presentation of the critical enablers and barriers to learning, sharing, and information management in the chemistry area.

7.3.2.3   Phase 3: requirements

Overview   Once the assessment phase was completed, the project team defined the requirements of the KM solution (or solutions). This meant creating a clear path for eliminating the gap between the current state and the desired state, as defined in the business case for action (project initiation phase). The steps for the requirement phase are outlined in Table 7.5.

Requirements process detail   Once the key barriers had been distilled, the team set about to develop solutions to address the barriers. From the work on the prototype, some solutions had already been identified as potential. In addition, other solutions were generated and then each was classified in terms of which barrier it was designed to overcome. Solutions were not limited to technology solutions but also included processes, new roles, changes in the organization, and the like.

Solutions were then classified according to which barrier they addressed, what the impact would be, what the effort would be to implement them, and what the time frame was for implementation and results. The final solutions were chosen based on whether they were medium to high impact or medium to low effort. Some change tasks

Table 7.5

Requirements Process

Phase 3: Requirements	
Process Steps	**Tools and Methods**

1. Determine solutions
  ▶ Draft possible solutions
  ▶ Review solutions with stakeholders
  ▶ Refine and prioritize solutions
  ▶ Present final solutions for approval
	▶ Discussion, brainstorming
	▶ Solution prioritization

2. Define system scope
  ▶ Content
  ▶ Function
  ▶ Audience
	▶ Project relationships
	▶ Design concepts
	▶ Metrics

3. Define resources scope
  ▶ Task schedule
  ▶ Resources schedule
  ▶ Budget
	▶ Requirements gathering
	▶ Task and resource schedules
	▶ Estimating techniques

4. Secure approval for project ▶ Adjust project scope or resources, if needed	▶ Steering committee meeting

were selected as "must-do," since they were critical to the implementation of any component of the project.

Seven "design" modules were selected and presented to the steering committee for approval, as follows:

1. *Project profile database:* a database and process for describing the specific details about each project currently underway, including team members, timelines, specific chemistry, biological action, and so on;

2. *Expertise directory:* an electronic directory of each chemist defining his or her schooling, areas of interest, publications, patents, and current projects (linked to project profile database);

3. *Notebook inventory:* a process for identifying areas in notebooks (both printed and electronic);

4. *Publishing learning opportunities:* a process for identifying what types of learning opportunities are available on a regular basis, including classes, seminars, conferences, mentoring, visitors, symposia, and so on.

5. *Scientific learning materials for new chemists:* computer-based materials specifically designed for new chemists to help them quickly begin producing at Lilly, including scientific and equipment resources, links to experts, policies and procedures, and so on.

6. *Combichem learning system:* an on-line collaborative system facilitated by expert chemists that teaches combinatorial chemistry in the context of the chemists' jobs and allows them to virtually partner on projects.

7. *Knowledge collaboration groups:* the processes for creating community exchange groups to allow chemists to brainstorm and share ideas about their work.

By the end of this phase, the project requirements were determined through working with subgroups of chemists and were ready for the design phase, during which each individual project would be more clearly defined in terms of process, roles, technologies, organizational changes, and support mechanisms.

7.4 Conclusion

In this chapter, we presented the OPPT framework as a general guide for a KM project and used the SPIN project to illuminate how this framework works. Specifically, we showed the first three phases of the KM system development process and a variety of tools and methods used in this project to help readers understand the front end of a KM project.

Knowledge is about transforming information to create value for an organization or a person. Knowledge management is about facilitating the process of transforming information to knowledge through better learning, sharing, and information management both at the individual and organizational levels. A KM system is not merely a repository of information. It is an arrangement of organization, people, process, and technology that is integrated for the purposes of knowledge transferring, sharing, and institutionalization. Therefore, developing a KM system has to take a holistic approach in which the favorable and unfavorable factors of these four constituents are taken into account.

Since knowledge is organic, however, so is a KM project. Every KM project is different, and so is its context. The enablers and barriers of each OPPT constituent are unique to each project and, consequently, KM solutions to address them differ. Our goal is not to assert one standard way of conducting a KM project. It is to share what we learned from our own experiences with the hope that readers can then gain valuable understanding and insight from our knowledge. This is KM.

References

[1]   Fahey, L., and L. Prusak. "The Eleven Deadliest Sins of Knowledge Management." *California Management Review* 40 (1998): 265–276.

[2]   Hansen, Morton, Nitin, Nohria and Thomas, Tierney. What's Your Strategy for Managing Knowledge?" *Harvard Business Review* 77 (1999): 106–116.

CHAPTER

8

Contents

The role of directories in KM

Michael L. Simpson

8.1 Background

As you already know, KM isn't just about information but information with added value. So there are two issues that must be dealt with, as follows:

1. How can your data and the supporting systems best support the addition of added value?

2. How do you add that value in the most efficient way?

Directories are not only an efficient tool for assisting in the advancement of your underlying network infrastructure to facilitate this move to KM, but they can also be the foundational method of daily interaction of people and systems. Let's start with establishing a definition for the traditional directory.

8.2   Problems with the traditional directory

Directories have been around as long as computer networking. Any networked application that is not for public use and requires you to discriminate access, has a database of users and associated passwords that together provide controlled access to the application. This database and basic authentication function is what most people consider a directory, but it really isn't a service until it extends beyond an individual application.

These single-purpose, application-specific directories are scattered about every computer network, including the Internet, and most companies have quite a few. In fact, numerous studies have determined that typical Fortune 500 corporations have on average well over 100 directories.

Since the information that is critical to employees doing their jobs is held and managed within myriad business applications, the directory, in even its simplest form, becomes critical to accessing and managing everyday tasks of communication and business. Therefore, efficiency is the first step to making the directory a tool, rather than a liability. How could it be a liability, you ask? Well, redundancy is the culprit. An average user has about 15 passwords and an average network has about 4,000 users.

That averages out to about 60,000 passwords that an IS department must provide administrative support for on a daily basis, and it creates a considerable amount of redundancy for employees. The typical network user regularly spends 44 hours per year logging in to network applications. What's more, 70 percent of all help-desk calls are related to forgotten passwords. Imagine if all this time could be used to actually get some work done.

We'll address methods of dealing with creating efficiencies throughout this chapter, and, yes, we will get to specific examples of KM applications that are based on directories; but it is important to first broaden your view of what a directory can be. Directories can positively impact the efficiency in interaction of people to people and even processes to processes, which is a far cry from merely the typical people to process (or application) role. An effective network focused on the needs of knowledge workers, rather than merely managing static data, must realize the benefits of a general-purpose, full-service directory.

Why, you ask? Well, just the impact of not integrating user account management from multiple applications can be devastating to a company, or at least quite costly. Let's say your vice president of worldwide sales quit three weeks ago and joined a competitor; and it seems someone didn't get around to removing this person's access to the sales database.

In the weeks that passed, your price list and information about all of your current accounts was in the hands of your greatest rival. Another common example is when one of your key employees responsible for purchasing goes on leave and others are covering his or her work. Since the rest of the organization is unaware, because the systems didn't reflect a change, by the time word gets around, inventories are low and bills are in arrears.

8.3 Full-service directory solution

The definition of a directory as a source of user information for the purposes of authentication and access control (what a user can do once he or she is authenticated to an application) is its most remedial role, but companies should not limit themselves to this. The directory has grown to be more of a general-purpose service, which begins with a logical representation of your network, your people, and all of your resources—from hardware in your infrastructure such as routers and PBXs to virtually every application and data source available.

Once the directory has knowledge of these entities and can graphically represent them in administration and user utilities, it can be used to facilitate the sharing of information between them for many, many purposes. After all, why should KM be limited to people? Of course, in the purest definition, KM requires intelligent people. But as devices and software become more intelligent, we must consider that for the knowledge worker to be effective, the network must take on much of the responsibility for basic tasks.

General-purpose directories began to emerge in the late 1990s to address the issues of not only reducing the redundancy in access to the multitude of available applications but also to provide configuration and management of devices, desktops, and many other types of applications.

They use many methods, such as dynamically synching data, redirecting the user account directory databases of applications, supporting open standards for data integration, and even single sign-on for proprietary applications. For the purposes of this book, we will first focus our attention on the directory-enabled access and data synchronization applications that people use to facilitate the location of individuals and information.

A good example that expresses the value most people can relate to is "the saga of the day after the quarterly password change." If you're like most people, when prompted to reset your password by one of your many applications, as you are quite regularly, you picked something easy to remember. Well, it was easy to remember yesterday, anyway. Today it seems you have drawn a blank, and thus you are reduced to putting yourself at the mercy of the help-desk waiting line.

With add-on single sign-on services, a general-purpose directory service can store passwords for many applications and synchronize data between them, thus alleviating the need for the user to remember and enter new passwords for each application. This greatly reduces help-desk calls, since most IT departments claim that the number one end-user request is for resetting forgotten passwords. Another benefit is the elimination of redundant tasks, such as logging in to the many applications you use each day. The cost savings can be immense. At one company I worked for, simply enabling four applications for single sign-on saved them almost $1 million a year in help-desk calls.

Now that directory services are expanding into other layers of the network beyond merely operating systems and applications, the vision of a fully integrated network is finally coming into reach.

8.3.1 Role of directory services

In a world where networks and people are focused on managing knowledge and not just devices and applications, some everyday technologies become even more critical. Directory services are right up there at the top of the list. There are three major areas for using directory technology, which, when used properly, can transform mere static information into dynamic, easily consumable knowledge. These three areas are as follows:

1. Finding knowledge workers;

2. Finding, filtering, and enhancing data;

3. Publishing and routing.

8.3.2 Building a directory foundation

The directory acts as the foundation of location, access, configuration, and management, as well as enabling new classes of applications that leverage these combined data. Any application that requires live information from multiple systems, rather than static representations, benefits greatly from a directory capable of acting as a clearinghouse of live data without requiring the application itself or a person to handle all the integration duties between data sources.

Built on top of this distributed knowledge database of every user, device, application, and service available inside and outside of your network is a policy management infrastructure. Few directories offer a policy management capability that can be used as a general engine for multiple applications and even people from multiple corporations over the Internet; but this will likely change in time, and more vendors will enter this lucrative market. Therefore, it's helpful to look at what is available and assume that options will increase.

What I mean by policy is likely more than you initially think, depending on whether you are approaching KM from the technical or the business point of view. But, as you are already discovering, true KM requires equal consideration of both. Some applications administer policies for the technical management of systems that control access, but most are quite limited. A few include policy definitions for role of the user; time of day; specific machine; method of authentication (biometric device, password, etc.); day of week; and PC resources such as memory, disk, video, and operating system version.

These types of policies can be applied to access and configuration of desktops, routers, switches, firewalls, and soon every device, service, and data source. It works tied to an event system. It is essentially a highly evolved "if-then" statement with associated processes. You can define a policy that says "if" a specific field of data is changed, then take x action, such as "change a, b, and c data" automatically. A good example is how Novell, Inc., integrated its own human resources database, PeopleSoft, with its directory and allowed the directory to handle the process for automating manual and multidepartmental events that changes in the HR database normally triggered.

What Novell found when it did an analysis of what happened when an employee was hired or removed from active working status was very interesting. Every action, of course, began with the human resources department, so it started there and did what is called "contextual inquiry." This is something all good IT departments should learn to do. Instead of merely asking HR what they wanted the software to do, it shadowed employees and took note of what they did in an average day. After gathering these data, the findings led to a few significant conclusions. There was enormous redundancy in daily tasks, there was not a consistent response from groups outside of HR that were involved in the process, and there was great room for human error because of the lack of managed process between employees.

You can probably relate to this dilemma. Have you ever changed jobs or locations within your own company or organization? You've likely experienced this many times. Well, based on these experiences, if you were to relocate today, would your expectation be that everything associated with your job would be fully functional the moment you arrived in your new location, or not? You're probably laughing out loud right now, or at least smirking a little—and with good reason. The process of information exchange between applications typically happens by what a few in the industry have come to call "the human gateway." With the example of Novell's HR department, you can see a good illustration.

What occurred daily in Novell's network when someone was hired or relocated was that the information was first entered in the HR database. Then, periodically, the HR employee created a report and e-mailed it to 27 people, who were each in charge of systems such as building security or telephony. Many of them had others in their group that needed to act on this information, so they told two friends, and so on and so on. Well, you get the picture. The information, after having been received in e-mail, was modified in the brain of the administrator of each system and came out in a different form in another application—thus, the human gateway.

Well, although this process has been used for many years, these gateways have a few problems. They do not all operate at the same speed, and some are very often overloaded with other processes to perform at an adequate response level. There is also very little error checking or process completion reporting in most of these systems, so the ultimate responsibility of reporting errors falls to the end user: the poor slob with a deadline from a new boss who is sitting in his or her brand new office completely shut off from the digital world. In short, people doing redundant tasks are fallible; but people are ultimately the key to making even an automated process work.

So Novell linked the HR processes with information in other systems that was regularly affected. When someone is added to the HR database and put on active status, that event is logged and a series of other events are triggered in external systems. The directory stores the rules, or policies, for what happens in each system, and external directory systems, gateways, and synchronization engines facilitate the processes. The result of Novell's using the directory to link processes in systems that have no real technical knowledge of each other has been quite profound. Today, when a new employee is hired, a network administrator is not even required 83% of the time. The 17% difference is when a particular employee's location, title, or status does not match the rules, such as a finance employee working in a field sales office rather than in the corporate facility.

The benefit for the user is even more profound. At the very moment the HR database is modified, the employee receives a user account in the directory that gives him or her access to the operating systems required to access department, location, and role. For example, if John Jones were hired in finance in San Jose, he would receive an identity that might reflect this fact—`jjones.finance.sanjose.novell`. Of course, he would rarely if ever be required to know that information, regardless of how intuitive it is. He would simply be, and be known as, John Jones. (See Figure 8.1.)

The system remembers what finance people in that location require, so static lists are no longer necessary. They need access to applications on NetWare, NT, and UNIX servers; remote dial-in to the local network; the secure, departmental printer; and the Internet. They also need Microsoft Office downloaded to their desktops and configured for them, an Internet browser, and access to the Oracle financials application. In the future,

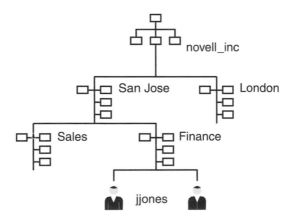

Figure 8.1   Linking the HR process.

they hope to add automatic creation of a building security badge and using integrated PBX technology, a phone extension and voice mail, all at the same time.

When users log in to their PCs, which have nothing on them but a directory access client and Microsoft Windows of some flavor, the directory identifies these users and requires them to change the password that HR assigned them. As a result, users spend about ten minutes downloading all the applications and configuration information, such as printer drivers and browser security settings, previously specified. After that, each user is completely operational and ready to start the day, hopefully without calling IT at all.

A great product to actually manage the people interaction of the process is called eProvision, by Business Layers, Inc. (www.businesslayers.com). eProvision builds upon the directory foundation and helps in assisting with the management of the process of provisioning services automatically. That's a helpful solution to get you off and running with a directory service and to help you build and maintain a foundational infrastructure of accurate information, but that's more of an efficiency model and you will want other knowledge-based solutions to build upon this base.

The good news is that with the appropriate directory service, all these systems can use the same foundational data and work together even if they weren't designed for any interoperability. By using the directory as the foundation for your infrastructure and knowledge-based applications, you can eliminate redundancy and greatly improve the accuracy of your information and, thus, the efficiency in how people interact with each other and use the information.

8.3.3   The human factor

There are also policies regarding how you do business that the technology must be aware of. You already define business policy through common processes—some manual and some embedded in your company's software. The key is to link these processes with your network infrastructure and with each other, without replacing or modifying them. One of the keys to creating a truly integrated network is understanding that the IT department isn't really in control. Many Its think that they are and consider themselves somewhat of a police force designed to protect users from themselves, but the reality is that an effective IT organization more often than not is a service organization. And service organizations will always be pushed into doing things they don't want to do, things that will eventually be difficult.

Take choosing applications, for instance. Often the IT organization is involved in the process, but the needs are determined by the department or organization that will daily be using the applications. Therefore, facts about which operating system, protocols, and development tools are best may be pushed aside for a specific feature or utility, and IT will just have to deal with the integration.

In that integration process, it is vitally important to understand who is the authoritative source of all data. What I mean is that in the process of integration, IT cannot expect to corral all data and become controllers, deciding who has access to what and where things are stored. For example, every department, such as human resources, finance, and security, has critical information that needs to remain protected and proprietary. IT must allay fears that by integrating information that should be shared, and enabling processes to happen automatically based on changes in those data, information and access will be compromised. In fact, proprietary information can even be used to trigger events in other systems, without revealing the original information.

The key is building a system that does not centrally assimilate the actual information; build a centralized policy manager who enables data to be controlled by the authoritative sources and, therefore, remain secure. Extensible Markup Language (XML) is the perfect technology to handle this, because it allows data to actually hold the information about how these data are displayed, as well as other rules that many applications can leverage, thus making these data more flexible and reusable without replication. This is done by using an XML-based integration service that leverages a full-service directory. Today they are rare, and choices are limited, but they may soon become commonplace as the XML market matures.

An XML-based directory solution allows you to create an application view of the information in the directory and then replicate that information via XML and an Extensible Stylesheet Language (XSL) processor. The solution preserves the authority of the data sources and is based completely on business policies for authority, mapping of information, and replication. You can access information from any disparate system without modifying the application, and you can then connect the information via an XML connector to the directory. Once in the directory you can then create a new type of cross-functional application, which can access a cross-section of the rich data set.

This completely eliminates the endless searching for data of relevance, and you can start fulfilling the requests of users to filter information for them, based on their current priorities. This enables companies to leverage the information that already exists throughout their enterprise and extend the value of application data by enabling cross-functional applications to take information from disparate systems and deliver new services.

Another factor to consider is that as more and more companies extend their business processes to the Internet, users will increasingly be accessing live information in their suppliers' and partners' networks, rather than static representations of that information in their own, physical network. As that happens, the amount of physical data that IT is in control of for some companies that have complex supply chains could end up being only 20% to 50% of the mission-critical information the company uses on a daily basis. When that occurs, what is IT's role?

Well, if IT doesn't manage the storage of information, then IT must evolve to managing policy and the quality of experience for users. ITs must take a more active role in filtering information for consumption by their users, based on policies that the users decide, not IT. The days of ITs being responsible for determining which applications, information, Web sites, and people are valuable are long gone.

We've covered how an automated process works to eliminate redundant tasks for employees, to free them up for higher-level work and to ensure that foundational people information is accurate and up-to-date; but you're probably wondering how a directory can be used with knowledge-based applications.

8.4   What to do next: finding knowledge workers

Well, people are the keepers of more knowledge than any system, and even with an integrated, full-service directory you can't, and wouldn't want to, replace them. So an important task for a chief knowledge officer is to ensure that customers can find the keepers of the knowledge as efficiently as possible. The first step is to locate the person, or data source, of the information you need.

It is easier when you know the location of the information and you can use basic Windows or Web-based search tools. The trick is when the data location is uncertain, or you only have partial information about a person, such as a first name.

8.4.1   Some other ideas

There are search tools, often known as corporate "white pages," from many vendors. There are even free utilities on the Web that are based on the lightweight directory access protocol (LDAP), which is the standard method of directory access. These utilities allow you to locate people with partial information. They can, and should, replace any paper corporate white pages. Check out www.novell.com/eGuide for a good example. Also, www.switchboard.com is built on a directory by Banyan, Inc., and is provided as a public service funded by advertising revenues.

Those that work best are built on a directory integrated with databases that are accurate and regularly updated. This is where live links to HR's systems would be helpful and should better explain why we spent so much time on that at the beginning of this chapter. A good rule to follow is go to the source, or your source will be wrong. In other words, if the accuracy of the information is not automatically controlled by the system that originally created it, the information will likely be inaccurate.

Therefore, perform the infrastructure integration up front or your knowledge system will have no foundation and may be more trouble than it is worth. Also, white pages applications that allow you to browse many different directories are best, because despite your most diligent efforts, it is unlikely that all of your data will ever be completely integrated, and you will likely never have only one directory. First seek to consolidate, but always be prepared to integrate when elimination of another directory is deemed impractical.

Another great solution is from Oblix, Inc. (www.oblix.com). They have two directory-based products that are extremely helpful. One is called the Oblix Workforce Automation Solution and the other is the Oblix Secure User Management Solution. The latter is more focused on identity management and is a great complement to the issues we discussed in the first half of the chapter.

The most applicable to the KM category is the Oblix Workforce Automation Solution. This product publishes your user information on-line and provides an intuitive Web-based interface so users can rapidly locate and contact the right individual or group of individuals based on name, role, title, reporting structure, or any other information you make available. It also enables users to securely update their own information, giving a greater likelihood that it is accurate.

But, although these search tools are helpful, they don't really give you a clue as to who really knows what you need. As you are well aware, someone's title is not the most accurate indication of what he or she knows, especially as you move up the corporate ladder. The keepers of the real knowledge are often not the managers, but rather those who deal with it in a practical manner every day. So how do you discern where they are and what they know?

Well, other than asking around, the typical method, there are intelligent systems built upon those same directories of user identities that actually learn people's skill sets and allow you to track them down. They move KM beyond merely finding the keepers of the knowledge and get straight into the information, without necessarily knowing who delivered it.

Structuring an eDirectory

The NDS eDirectory is a shrink-wrapped, off-the-shelf product. Users do not have to create a "roll their own" solution, thus avoiding the need to develop the entire content personalization application and subsequent maintenance. NDS eDirectory offers scheduled updates and maintenance releases.

NDS eDirectory is a fully distributed, manageable, and replicated directory. All directory servers can hold the same data. As a result, service continues if any directory server happens to fail. For most organizations, this is a major benefit to mission-critical reliability.

NDS replication also gives the flexibility to write to any copy of the directory. Many other directories are architected such that you have to update to a specific directory where the user profile information is stored. This results in a single point of failure that doesn't occur with NDS. Additionally, replication gives NDS eDirectory the ability to distribute the load of both reads and writes to the directory. NDS eDirectory has the ability to manage a billion objects without any performance degradation—in effect, unlimited growth.

Even with millions of objects added to the directory, NDS eDirectory performs LDAP search queries with consistent speed. The systems provide flexibility in terms of personalizing content for different groups of users, including the concept of using auxiliary classes. It is known as a standalone, cross-platform LDAP directory service that provides e-businesses with a foundation for growth, letting them easily build and securely maintain highly customized e-relationships, quickly deploy leading-edge e-business services, and deliver fast, personalized content. [1]

8.4.2 Finding, accessing, and filtering knowledge

With the endless amount of available data, it's almost impossible to determine who to ask and what is of value. Companies spend countless wasted hours with employees redundantly searching for the same information and often finding that the information is inaccurate or at least old enough to make you question its applicability. There are many directory-based applications available that can help ease this burden.

A great example is a product by Orbital, Inc. (www.orbitalsw.com) called Organik. Organik provides users with a simple, yet powerful way to quickly and easily get answers to questions, either by searching previously recorded questions and answers or by submitting their questions to experts. Users can also use Organik to find people with particular types of expertise, experience, or interests. Organik creates profiles, which they call "Personas," of the people in the community or organization and uses these to allow users to find answers to questions or to find people with particular skills and knowledge.

Users submit their questions to Organik, which then attempts to answer the question from previously captured and stored conversations. If Organik cannot provide a suitable answer from the existing database, it automatically identifies and routes the question to several predetermined experts. Organik selects these experts by matching the question against its store of expert Personas, built on the basis of experts' ongoing Q&A participation with Organik and their current user rating (you get to rate the quality of the answer).

A great place to see their software in action is www.answers.com. Answers.com is an Internet site, but the technologies used underneath, Organik and Novell's eDirectory, are used in corporations around the world for similar purposes.

Another user of eDirectories is Phoenix, Arizona–based ON Semiconductor [2], which had about 100 directories, each of which was like an isolated silo in an extensive landscape. Even with business as usual, keeping 100 separate directories updated in a cohesive manner was laborious and complicated by large-scale divestments, mergers, and acquisitions. The company recognized this data duplication and synchronization problem and knew that a directory was the thing that could solve the problem; it wanted to reduce the number of places it had to maintain employee and contractor profiles.

Another requirement was integrated profile maintenance across heterogeneous Windows/UNIX environments from a single point. As a multinational company with a diverse network and with a plan for enabling new applications and streamlining inherited processes, the company wanted a product that would serve as a springboard for advanced capabilities such as single sign-on, PKI, and digital certificate management.

8.4.3 Publishing knowledge

Now that you have gone through the process of gathering the knowledge that helped you do your job, you need to publish it for the benefit of others. The line between mere data and knowledge can blur a bit here because we often consider data as static information, which would imply that data are contained in a document. Well, this is no longer the case. With the help of directories, we can create documents that are actually "alive." Alive in the sense that they are constantly changing and enabling you to spend less time tracking down people and more time doing your job.

Since your directory, if linked to live data from your critical applications, is available to all your users and maintains accurate information, it is a great place to handle the publishing of information and mange the interaction between people. One of the first steps in the use of directories that give you a glimpse of the role they will play in the future of KM is the evolution of the paper form. Extinction may be more accurate. Since the directory understands the role of all people, and controls security unique to them, processing forms and approvals using the directory is quite logical.

A new company called Jetforms (www.jetforms.com) is focused on this space and can enable you to enhance your processes. One example is with a very simple process of travel authorization. A user fills out an online form. The bulk of the data for the travel request is automatically pulled out of the user's profile in the directory and the form is filled out, awaiting the user to enter the travel dates and purpose. Once that is done, the form is automatically sent outside the company to the outsourced travel agency, and the pricing and availability are determined.

The form is then routed to the requesting employee's boss for approval and then back to the employee if rejected or to the travel agency if approved.

8.5 Conclusion

The previous example is an illustration of keeping information secure whether it changes hands inside or outside of your company. Since you can design forms for any purpose you like, you can make the information sharing and even simple publishing quite dynamic. No longer are you required to design complex systems for collaboration of simple documents for short-term projects. Now you can on the fly design live documents that enable people to customize or change some information and only view other fields. These types of directory-based applications make great filters into large data sources to optimize the interaction of people.

The directory is the foundational key to integration of people, processes, and information. It will be the source for locating and interacting with knowledge workers and even automate the sharing of knowledge. For a directory to reach its potential, it must first know who it's serving; you must seek to find a justifiable method to gather knowledge of all the people and as many of their devices and applications as you can inside the directory. I say justifiable because it is unlikely that everyone in your company will understand or even care about your vision of a fully integrated, knowledge-based network.

After all, how many times has every organization or department of your enterprise implemented, without argument, and on time, any technology that was mandated? Therefore, you must look for a short-term return on investment (ROI) through any applications or services that gather user information and identities into the directory.

On-line corporate white pages, desktop management, software distribution, and public key infrastructure (PKI) are common Internet and messaging technologies for security; they are all good candidates because each may touch every employee and provide a tangible value for users and department heads. Once you get the user data, and hopefully applications, you can begin to build on this base. The good news is that with a flexible system, you need not redesign and redeploy if your needs change through time.

References

[1]   www.Novell.com.

[2]   *Network Magazine*, December 5, 2000.

9

Contents

The Internet as a mechanism to enhance content and extend access to corporate data resources

Larry L. Learn

9.1 Background

The Internet can be an extremely valuable asset when it comes to data warehousing [1]. Properly structured, the Internet can provide a superb window on the data warehouse assembled by the enterprise, allowing extensive, economical, and timely access, using a nearly ubiquitous access platform (e.g., a Web browser), by enterprise members from nearly anywhere on the planet [2]. It can also serve as a viable mechanism to economically integrate database elements of a distributed data resource.

This is particularly true where trading partners have joined elements of their respective corporate data resources to support mutual goals and objectives, where organizations have merged or formed joint ventures, or where the organization is geographically dispersed—particularly internationally. However, enterprise data warehouses—even with the combined resources of multiple organizations—often fall far short of meeting the greater information needs of an organization in a timely manner. This is where the Internet can really step up to plate and score in a big way. It is this aspect of the role of the Internet in augmenting the systematic information resources of the enterprise—its total data warehouse—that will be the primary focus of this chapter.

9.1.1 Size, scope, and rate of growth of the Web

Recent research [3] indicates that the size of the World Wide Web comprises approximately 3.6 million Web sites. About 2.2 million of these sites are thought to be public in nature (i.e., to offer unrestricted access to nontrivial information content), containing in excess of 286 million [4] Web pages. The current productive Web data store is somewhere in the neighborhood of 35,000 GB to 59,000 GB (i.e., 35–59 terabytes). The overall number of sites increased by around 800,000 between 1997 and 1998, a 65% increase. The increase is found to be closer to 53% in 1998–1999, suggesting that while the growth in these public Web sites continues in absolute numbers, the rate of growth—while still very large—is slowing somewhat [5].

The average size of a Web site in 1999 was 129 pages, compared with 114 pages in 1998—a 13% increase. In 1998, the number of Web pages on public sites was approximately 166 million, while by 1999 this total had increased by about 120 million pages (i.e., a total of upwards of 286 million pages). As a comparison, the Library of Congress adds around 10,000 items to its collection each working day—around 2.6 million items (approximately 650 million pages) each year. Clearly, regardless of the metric used, the size, scope, and makeup of the Web are highly dynamic and growing rapidly.

Some experts might beg to differ with these precise numbers (or their interpretation); nonetheless, it is evident that there is a huge—and ever growing—resource of valuable and timely information available from the Web for little or no cost and effort. And when the prospect of information for payment (or in many instances, simply registering with the Web site) is also included, this potential information resource significantly increases in size, scope, and value. But more important than the scope and size of this resource is both its "currency" (i.e., timeliness or newness) and the timely, ubiquitous, and economic access to this resource the Web affords. These are without a doubt the most valuable aspects of the Internet information resource.

9.1.2   Information gold mine

There is hardly an area of culture, government, education, or commerce that is not already richly represented with vast amounts of valuable information resources somewhere on the Internet.

These resources include agricultural data, technical data, medical and scientific data, legal and judicial data, regulatory data, patent and trademark data, securities and financial data, current news and weather, competitor information, and so on—just to name a few arbitrary categories. And, as we have seen, the resources are growing by significant amounts both in scope and scale of contention on a daily basis. Frequently, this information is simply available for the taking as a true information gold mine.

But rather than locking the information away for only the use of an elite set of researchers who must travel to the physical source of the information, cyberspace makes the information conveniently and ubiquitously available from almost any location around the world. However, unlike a typical library, which provides many direct and indirect mechanisms for professional intermediation (e.g., professional librarians, refereed scholarly journals), cyberspace can provide far greater problems in locating and evaluating pertinent information resources.

9.2   Problems with information overload

The volume of viable information on the Internet can be both a blessing and a curse. Even after obviously nonrelevant, untimely, unverifiable, or inappropriate information has been weeded from the results of an Internet search (e.g., using one of many Web search engines: WebCrawler, Yahoo!, AltaVista, Excite, Lycos, MetaCrawler, NBCi), too often what remains can still be daunting. The techniques of classifying (e.g., the use of such information classification schemes as the Dewey Decimal System: http://www.oclc.org/oclc/fp/index.htm), inventorying, and qualifying information on the Internet are still in their infancy.

More often than not, when embarking upon the quest to obtain a particular facet of knowledge from the Internet (i.e., to "mine" the Internet), the problem is not so much one of finding related information. It becomes one of sorting through vast amounts of relevant (and too often, irrelevant) results and attempting to determine both the timeliness and veracity of the information that has been found.

While the Internet has become the great democratizing agent of information and knowledge presentation, it is this very facet of the Internet that has also created the opportunity for vast amounts of information to be made widely available. This is with little regard for delineating either the reliability of the knowledge or information source, or the authority and timeliness of the knowledge itself and, too often, without due consideration for structure or organization. It is this missing validation, organization, and structure that currently diminishes the value of this vast information resource to most organizations. But this need not be a reason for the organization to ignore this wealth of valuable and current information, and, hopefully, this problem will itself be diminished over time.

9.2.1 Missing structure

While the enterprise data warehouse is generally characterized by the elements of structure that have been carefully incorporated within it [6], the unrefined information resources available on the Internet are most often characterized by their very lack of structure; they are often simply static HTML (i.e., Web) documents [7]. Fortunately, there are ways to at least begin to impose some aspect of needed structure on access to these Internet information resources from within the enterprise environment.

To effectively exploit the Internet, it is useful (if not essential) to possess (or to have at one's ready disposal) appropriate tools or utilities constructed and maintained by a person or persons who possess the following skills:

1. A general understanding of what information might be available in cyberspace;

2. A general knowledge of where and how to approach locating the desired information;

3. A complement of effective tools, such as search engines, and other resources, such as booklists; for sifting out the "gold" from the "silt and sand";

4. A recognition that when mining the Internet, unlike other more familiar information or knowledge resources, one must take additional care to qualify the results (i.e., caveat emptor).

Fortunately, once plowed, this fertile ground need not be repeatedly plowed by every member of the enterprise seeking the same information. Just as the classical library can provide the tools and organization (i.e., structure) that enable the common information seeker to find desired, current, and authoritative information in an adequate and timely manner, there are also techniques that begin to mold the extensive, and often unqualified and unrefined, information resources of the Internet into a valuable and structured information warehouse. As we will see, metadata can provide at least some degree of added structure and simplify productive access to information from the Web.

9.2.2 Metadata: adding missing structure

Simply stated, metadata are data about data [8]. While the term may not be familiar to some readers, the concept most likely is very familiar. An example of metadata might be the familiar card in the library card catalog. Actually, metadata are the information printed on the card, but this is probably an irrelevant distinction for purposes of this presentation.

And if you are not old enough to remember the row upon row of drawers filled with library cards that in the past provided the primary means of access to the collection of books and other resources in the library, you may be familiar with the microfiche catalog or the computer terminal used now in many libraries to display the same information. Metadata are the background information that describes the content, quality, condition, and other appropriate characteristics of these data.

Upon reflection, the existence of physical library cards, microfiche copies, or discrete electronic computer records, which comprised the classical library catalog, had more to do with the physical nature of the book and the inability of the information seeker to have easy physical access to the entirety of the information collection than with the information contained on the cards themselves. The physical library card catalog had nothing to do with any basic requirement for the separation of the book from the metadata carrier (e.g., the card itself). In fact, in an electronic infrastructure, there is little necessity to physically separate metadata from the information resource itself. More simply stated, metadata content can be (and probably should be) contained within the related electronic information resource (i.e., metatags). But essentially the question is, what information might be used to best describe the specific information resource?

9.2.3 Dublin Core

For information in electronic form (e.g., Web-based data), much effort has been expended to answer this very question, and one answer—and the answer that seems to be gaining consensus support on the Web—is the "Dublin Core" [9], so called because it resulted from a broad-based effort in a meeting hosted by Online Computer Library Center, Inc. (OCLC), in Dublin, Ohio.

A detailed foray into the depths of the Dublin Core is clearly beyond the scope of this book. The basic constituent elements of the Dublin Core include title, subject, author, publisher, other agent (e.g., significant contributor other than the author), date, object type (e.g., poem, spreadsheet, picture, film clip), form (ASCII text, HTML, PDF, etc.), identifier (e.g., URL, PURL), source (object—either print or electronic—from which this object is derived), language, relation (relationship to other objects), and coverage (the spatial locations and temporal durations characteristic of the object) [10]. Not surprisingly, this is very reminiscent of the type of information contained on the more familiar library catalog card.

When metadata are imbedded into electronic documents using an established (i.e., standard) structure—for example, Resource Description Framework (RDF), Standard Generalized Markup Language (SGML), or XML—a consistent structure is introduced that enables automated retrieval of selective information.

Stated in more familiar terms, accurate metadata incorporated within the documents themselves, in a known and systematic way, enable identification, selection, and authentication of documents across the network, using automated techniques, in a manner very much analogous to the use of the card catalog in a classical library setting. As we will see, this can facilitate the automated harvesting of information from the Web using Information Robots (Infobots).

Unfortunately, since the author(s) of the Web page controls the inclusion of metadata in the documents, erroneous or misleading metadata can be surreptitiously included to purposefully misdirect access attempts. This is a particularly rampant problem where, for example, pornographic Web site owners have included copious quantities of misleading metadata to cause search engines to present their site in response to completely unrelated legitimate search queries.

From a practical perspective, the Web is still a long way from making the majority of its information available with adequate embedded metadata. Strides are being made, and an understanding of the technologies will likely prove invaluable in planning and developing future data warehouse infrastructures that begin to encompass the vast information or knowledge resources available on the Web. Meanwhile, these techniques can be very productively employed in the construct of the enterprise data warehouse.

9.3   Solutions: harvesting the Internet

The size of the Web makes it practically impossible to search even a miniscule subset of the entirety of the available information manually. This has given rise to the invention of automated methods of seeking out relevant information. While an in-depth discussion of these entities (i.e., Infobots) is beyond the scope of this chapter, a brief overview is clearly worthwhile. Information automatons, called variously Web Robots, Infobots, Web Crawlers, Web Spiders, and so on, are utilized for a number of important and useful functions on the Internet, including (but not limited to) the following:

1. *Statistical analysis:* discovering the total number of Web servers, average number of documents per Web server, average page size, and so on

2. *Maintenance:* identifying and removing "dead" or "broken" links [11]

3. *Mirroring:* making a copy of portions (or the entirety) of an already existing Web site resource

4. *Resource discovery:* searching out specific information or specific types of information on the Web

Since Infobots, to varying degrees, utilize valuable computer resources and telecommunications bandpass associated with the Web sites they visit, many server maintainers (understandably) do not want this excessive load or, for other reasons, do not want robots accessing their server, or parts thereof. One method chosen in practice [12] by server maintainers to address this issue is the creation of a file called robots.txt, placed in a known location on the server, that contains an access policy for robots. This is clearly a voluntary procedure, but experience relates that most robot operators do indeed respect the wishes of the Web server maintainer in this regard. In this way, the page owner can decide to specify which parts of the URL space should be avoided by robots.

This file can also be used to warn robots of "black holes" (areas of the Web that are extraordinarily large or complicated) [13]. Related information may also be specified with metadata contained in a Web page. Metadata included in Web pages can aid Infobots that are designed to take advantage of this mechanism and to harvest more relevant data when engaged in resource discovery activities. In addition, important information can be conveyed to visiting Infobots regarding Web site policies and other relevant information related to the specific Web site visited.

Recently, Infobots (as well as other means of access to external Web sites) have come under legal fire.

In attempts to deter unauthorized use of an organization's computer and network resources by other organizations, allegations of Trespass of Chattels, a legal concept that protects the property of an organization or individual for its own use, have been asserted with some success in the U.S. courts [14]. A legal opinion obtained by me regarding this issue suggests that the existing case(s) will likely be overturned upon appeal and the courts will hold that such activities are "diminimus," and the customary use of Internet links is allowed under the law. However, this is only a prospective opinion, and the courts, of course, will have the final word.

While Infobots are a fruitful technical tool for the information professional, in the light of these recent legal developments, it is advised that their use be scrutinized by appropriate legal expertise.

9.3.1   Broken links

The most common mechanism for identifying information resources on the Internet is the Uniform Resource Locator, or URL. But the URL is not a fixed identifier, and it can change at the whim of a hardware reconfiguration, file system reorganization, or changes in organizational structure, often resulting in the dreaded "404—Document Not Found" error message.

This is akin to the situation that existed at one time in the telephone network, when telephone numbers were assigned on the basis of the physical wire that led to a subscriber's house. If the subscriber moved, the previous telephone number was no longer valid (at least for the original subscriber), and knowledge of a new number was required to phone that subscriber.

This all changed with the advent of local number portability (LNP). In the modern telephone network, the actual physical number that identifies the wire leading to a subscriber's residence is often unknown to all but the local telephone carrier. The published number (i.e., telephone number given out by the subscriber or published in a phone directory) is merely a "token" representing the physical number.

To obtain the physical number, the telephone company goes to a computerized database and looks up the corresponding physical number before completing a call. This enables the subscriber, in general, to keep a particular published number regardless of how many times he or she moves.

As we will see, one mechanism—the so-called Persistent Uniform Resource Locator, or PURL [15]—to minimize the problem of broken links (i.e., no longer valid URL for a given document) is very similar in concept to LNP. While not eliminating the problem itself (i.e., the changing URL), the goal is to stabilize the reference point to a given document.

This must be done to the extent that everyone in an organization (or in the broader cyberspace) seeking that document does not find it necessary to spend time and energy tracking down the new URL. In fact, the responsibility for maintaining the integrity of the PURL is often assumed by the document owner, making the URL change transparent to the document seeker. This can make the concept of PURLs particularly valuable when designing the Internet enterprise data warehouse. It is interesting to note that the PURL itself can be considered metadata, since it is information about information (i.e., the current URL of the Web page being sought).

9.3.2   PURLs of wisdom

Before tackling PURLs in greater detail, a brief synopsis of related terminology is in order. The so-called Uniform Resource Identifier (URI) is the generic set of all names/addresses that are short strings referring to resources. The Uniform Resource Locator (URL) is the set of URI schemes that have explicit instructions on how to access the resource on the Internet.

The Uniform Resource Name (URN) is a URI that has an institutional commitment to persistence, availability, and so on. (Note that this sort of

URI may also be a URL.) The PURL is an example (although not the only example) of a URN. To aid in the development and acceptance of URN technology, a naming and resolution service for general Internet resources has been developed [16]. The names, which are referred to as Persistent URLs (PURLs), can be used in documents, Web pages, and in cataloging systems. PURLs increase the probability of correct resolution over that of URLs and thereby reduce the burden and expense of maintaining viable, long-term access to electronic resources.

A PURL is actually a URL. But rather than pointing directly to the location of an Internet resource, a PURL uses an HTTP redirect (i.e., similar to the LNP application discussed previously) to point to an intermediate resolution service. This then associates the PURL with the actual URL and returns that URL to the client application, which can then complete the URL transaction in the normal manner. PURLs provide the means to assign a name for a network resource that is persistent, even if the item changes its actual location. For instance, when a Web resource is referred to by the PURL, only a single change to the PURL database is required if the resource later moves, and occurrences of the PURL contained in documents across the Web (e.g., portals, bookmark lists in enterprise members' workstation browsers) will remain valid. If properly maintained, the PURL will always point to the current location of the resource, no matter where it is.

It is important to note that persistence is a function of organizations, not technology. It is expected that a PURL service will always be available to resolve the PURL [17].

When a Web present element of an enterprise data warehouse is created and assigned a PURL, that data element will persist and be accessible using that PURL regardless of how many times the physical location (i.e., common URL) of that document may change, provided the PURL is maintained. To maintain a PURL, the maintainer may be a registered user of an established PURL resolution service. However, software for such a service has been placed into the public domain [18] and may be downloaded via the Internet [19]. Hence, an organization can also establish and maintain its own PURL resolution service.

9.3.3   Protecting the Internal Data warehouse: security concerns

It is necessary, in order to take advantage of the information resources available on the Internet, to establish a connection to the Internet. However, in connecting to the Internet, the enterprise must accept and manage new risks and threats to its internal resources.

The very nature of the Internet is nearly ubiquitous, international in scope and scale, open to the public, and without many (if not most) of the inherent controls that managers have come to expect when dealing with internal networks. This makes it imperative to consider protecting internal information resources and systems from deleterious external attacks. Firewalls and other policies are typically used in an attempt to address these problems.

It is probably most valuable for the information manager within an enterprise to recognize that, as the term wall implies, mechanisms designed to prevent intrusions are merely obstacles of a given height imposed between the outside world and the internal information resources.

There are no perfect firewalls of which I am aware. Firewalls simply raise the bar to such an extent that they discourage intruders, based on the knowledge and ability of the interloper and upon the resource and dedication such a person, or group of people, can bring to bear on an effort to penetrate a system. While implementing a firewall will deter some illicit attempts to gain access to the internal resources, the manager must realize that these resources are still vulnerable to penetration by those who might have the determination, expertise, and resources to scale the finite height of the firewall that has been implemented. Implementing more sophisticated—and generally more costly—firewall technology will only raise the bar.

Regardless of the sophistication (and the cost) of a firewall, it still can only create a wall of finite (although possibly very great) height and will still not be invulnerable. The only truly perfect protection is to put the system in a secure and impenetrable vault and lock the door—an impractical solution. Therefore, firewalls should be only one part of a strategy to minimize risks from external attacks and to protect the internal information resources.

Virtual private network (VPN) connections are recommended where the Internet is utilized to interconnect distributed elements of the enterprise data warehouse, or where the Internet is utilized as an access mechanism from remote enterprise users. VPNs provide an armored tunnel (e.g., cloaked and encrypted) through the public infrastructure and are another recommended mechanism to further protect this valuable resource. VPN technology can be utilized between interconnected servers [20] or within commonly used PC workstation operating systems [21].

Since VPNs can only protect data in transit through the protected channel, it is necessary to carefully assess vulnerabilities at both ends of the tunnel. For example, a workstation on the Internet can establish an armored channel (i.e., VPN) between the workstation and the enterprise data warehouse. This means—if the workstation itself is not provided with an adequate firewall—it remains vulnerable to penetration from the Internet and an interloper can easily commandeer the workstation to subsequently gain access to the enterprise data warehouse using the secure VPN channel.

As more remote enterprise users (e.g., telecommuters, casual work-at-home users) seek higher bandpass solutions to remote access, many are moving to digital subscriber line (xDSL), integrated services digital network (ISDN), and broadband cable modem access mechanisms. It should be noted that these technologies typically provide not only improved bandpass, but can also augment opportunities for illicit access to files contained on the user's home computer—particularly where "open door" network policies are allowed.

Enterprise users (particularly cable-modem users) should be warned of these increased risks and provided with related security information (e.g., restricting file sharing within Windows 95). Commercial firewall software packages are also available to help address these enhanced security risks.

9.3.4   Internal security risks

Although threats to the enterprise data store are most often considered in terms of pernicious actions and events that have their origins outside the realm of the organization itself, threats that occur from inside the organization, which can (and often do) cause equally deleterious outcomes, are too often overlooked or ignored. Internal threats most frequently involve inadvertent events, such as innocent human error, software failure, equipment failure, environmental factors, or physical disasters, which can be just as destructive as those perpetrated by external forces.

Disgruntled employees (or ex-employees) are also common sources of internally generated deleterious outcomes. Externally generated security risks should certainly be appropriately addressed, but addressed as yet another element in an overall security and risk avoidance/mitigation program, which includes an analysis and accommodation of potential internal threats as well. This should include an initial need for access analysis before granting a particular level of access authority, periodic access authority reviews, appropriate password control and review, access authentication, prompt revocation of access upon termination or transfer, and so on.

9.3.5 Controlling egress

When implementing access to the Internet, enterprise managers often wish to establish various controls on the scope of external resources that are made available to internal users. As we have seen, firewalls create a barrier to unwanted access from outside the enterprise perimeter, with the effectiveness of that barrier (i.e., the height of the wall) generally determined by the effort and resources an enterprise is willing to devote to this function.

Many of the same principles apply when attempting to control egress from within the perimeter of the enterprise (i.e., access to information that is outside the perimeter of the enterprise). While there are a variety of technical approaches to controlling egress (e.g., proxies, DNS servers, firewalls, and so on), the exact technical configuration used to monitor and control egress is most often best determined by the physical and logical configuration of the enterprise network itself. The logical concepts will be our focus.

In most applications, there are two basic approaches used to control, as compared with to monitor egress from the local network by enterprise users. These approaches are as follows:

1. A database (i.e., list) of allowed URLs that an enterprise user is permitted to visit;

2. A database of forbidden URLs that an enterprise user is not allowed to visit.

This process is generally referred to as URL filtering. These databases are usually determined by management policies established within the enterprise. Unfortunately, considerable human resources can be consumed in the attempt to create and maintain these databases on a day-to-day basis.

Fortunately, a number of vendors provide hardware, system resources, and basic database(s), which enterprise management can either implement as provided or enhance to meet specific enterprise policies, usually with considerably less effort than would be required to construct and maintain the database from scratch. In addition, the various vendors frequently provide a database maintenance and update service—typically for a fee.

Another approach relies on the identification of certain key words or phrases, contained either in the outgoing query or within the content of the returned results. Unfortunately, this approach can sometimes lead to unwanted consequences—either not restricting external access where this might be desired or, more often, unduly restricting access where such access might be desirable. As a very simple example, keying off the word "sex" might be intended to restrict access to sexually oriented content, but this might also restrict access to content regarding "sex discrimination," "sexual harassment," demographic market information using the sex of the consumer (i.e., male or female), and so on. Generally speaking, many enterprises find this approach to be nonproductive.

As organizations attempt to control egress, they often discover that a significant portion of their traffic is targeted on a reasonably small subset of allowed URLs. Or, similarly, where a deny strategy is adopted, an identifiable set of URLs may receive significant numbers of references by internal users.

Regardless of egress control strategies, this phenomenon frequently presents the opportunity for an organization to both improve performance and reduce expensive external bandpass utilization by local caching of content [22] from these high-activity URLs. Some commercially available systems commonly deployed to provide egress control also can provide these caching services. Regardless of whether an organization deploys egress control technology, it may be worthwhile investigating the further utility of caching functionality (sometimes called internet accelerators or proxies).

9.4   What to do next by monitoring egress

Recording and auditing (i.e., monitoring, rather than directly restricting) external resources visited can sometimes be more productive. Often vendor-provided systems create a database of external resources visited. Frequently, utility software is also provided with the system (or the database is designed to be compatible with commonly available applications, such as Microsoft Access) that can be utilized to sort accesses by user, by resource visited, and so on, and generate management reports.

This information can be useful in building or enhancing pass or deny URL lists, assisting management in establishing or revising access policies, or enabling management to take specific remedial actions when potential abuse by a specific enterprise user is uncovered.

Routinely monitoring bandpass utilization on external telecommunications channels can often be worthwhile as well and is highly recommended. While this methodology, in and of itself, seldom provides specific user access information, it can be a very good indicator of changes in general user behavior or overall enterprise resource expenditure directed toward utilization of outside resources (e.g., bandpass trending).

This approach is sometimes used by management, in conjunction with more precise reporting and auditing, as a trigger to alert management to the potential need to take a closer or more timely look at more specific utilization data using other (e.g., reporting and auditing) techniques. Routine bandpass monitoring can sometimes provide a tip-off to firewall penetration as well.

As an antidotal example, such monitoring tipped off one large company to surreptitious activities after hackers penetrated the company firewall and established an FTP directory on one of the company's computers. The interlopers subsequently uploaded illegal software to this directory and then posted the URL on a clandestine bulletin board.

Word quickly spread, and literally hundreds of Internet users were soon accessing this directory, resulting in a significant increase in the company's bandpass utilization. This increase was soon noted, and the company was able to identify and correct the problem in record time.

9.4.1 Network storage

Network-resident storage devices have been around for some time and are often utilized as a centralized mechanism for backing up network-resident workstations, servers, or other devices that include local data storage.

With the evolution of very high speed local area network technology (e.g., Fibre Channel [23]), and with ever-increasing demands for 7-day/24-hour operation, high availability, and ever more demanding performance requirements, many organizations have moved support of their on-line storage onto network-resident storage servers.

As broadband telecommunications facilities have become more economical and more widely available, this technology has also come into use to facilitate backing up (often dynamically) enterprise data stores in a remote location for purposes of emergency disaster recovery.

While this technology can have many useful applications in more common data warehousing infrastructures, it can also productively come into play using evolving broadband Internet connections. With the evolution of gigabit-class Internet connections (e.g., Internet2 [24]), this technology holds the promise of becoming a driving force in future data warehouse strategies.

The Internet2 Distributed Storage Infrastructure (I2-DSI) is a replicated hosting service for Internet content and applications across a distributed infrastructure consisting of servers with substantial processor and storage resources. Each user request is directed to the server closest to the requesting client. In this manner, network traffic is kept local and load is balanced among the distributed servers. This technology can form the basis for a distributed data warehouse application using the Internet.

9.5   Conclusion

The Internet provides an effective and economic mechanism to interconnect geographically dispersed elements of a distributed data warehouse resource. It also provides a convenient, effective, and economical mechanism to provide access to the enterprise data warehouse by geographically dispersed (e.g., remote) enterprise data users. But by far the most valuable facet of the Internet is the enormous, rich, and timely information or knowledge resource it can bring to the enterprise, either as an element or augmentation to the existing data warehouse resources of an organization.

The material in this chapter provides a high-level discussion of these valuable available assets—opportunities as well as potential pitfalls—endowed with a rich array of supporting resources contained in the references to provide further insight to specific areas of reader interest.

It was specifically designed to provide fertile soil, and to plant viable seeds that might enable the Knowledge Manager to nurture and grow, using the Internet, an effective and valuable new or expanded enterprise resource that might significantly enhance enterprise productivity and lead to demonstrable improvement in bottom-line results.

References

[1] Vivek R. Gupta, *An Introduction to Data Warehousing:* (Gupta defines: "A data warehouse is managed data situated after and outside the operational systems."); http://www.system-services.com/dwintro.asp.

[2] Larry L. Learn, "The Impact of the Internet on Enterprise Networks," in *The Network Manager's Handbook.* 3rd ed., ed. John M. Lusa (Auerbach, NY: CRC Press, 1999), 203. http://www.auerbach-publications.com.

[3] Brian F. Lavoie, Web Characterization Project Analyzes Net Content," *OCLC Newsletter* 242 (November/December 1999): 22; http://oclc.org/oclc/new/n242/index.htm.

[4] Don Clark, "Inktomi Promises Improved Searches for Customers after Study of the Web," *The Wall Street Journal—Interactive Edition* (January 18, 2000). (According to this study, the number of Web pages may currently exceed 1 billion, but these include many pages that may not have content suitable for use within the enterprise.) http://interactive.wsj.com.

[5] Lavoie, op. cit.

[6] Richard Tanler, "Putting the Data Warehouse on the Intranet" (May 1996); http://www.dbmsmag.com/9605i08.html.

[7] Hyper Text Markup Language (HTML), RFC 1866; http://www.faqs.org/rfcs/rfc1866.html.

[8] David Hart et al., "Metadata Primer—A 'How to' Guide on Metadata Implementation"; http://www.lic.wisc.edu/metadata/metaprim.htm.

[9] "Dublin Core Metadata Element Set: Reference Description"; http://www.oclc.org:5046/oclc/research/conferences/dc6/dces.html.

[10] "Dublin Core Metadata Element Set . . . ," op. cit.

[11] R. T. Fielding, "Maintaining Distributed Hypertext Infostructures: Welcome to MOMspider's Web." First International Conference on the World Wide Web, Geneva, Switzerland, May 25–27, 1994, 147–156; http://www1.cern.ch/PapersWWW94/fielding.ps.

[12] M. Koster, "A Standard for Robot Exclusion"; http://info.Webcrawler.com/mak/projects/robots/exclusion.html.

[13] Robots, op. cit.

[14] Carl S. Kaplan, "Tough Times for Data Robots," *The New York Times (on the Web)* (January 12, 2001); http://www.nytimes.com/2001/01/12/technology/12CYBERLAW.html.

[15] Stuart Weibel et al., "PURLs: Persistent Uniform Resource Locators"; http://purl.oclc.org/OCLC/PURL/SUMMARY.

[16] Keith Shafer et al., "Introduction to Persistent Uniform Resource Locators"; http://purl.oclc.org/OCLC/PURL/INET96.

[17] Ibid.

[18] OCLC Online Computer Library Center, Inc., Dublin, OH; http://www.oclc.org/.

[19] PURL Resolution Service software has been placed into the public domain by OCLC, Inc., and is available free of charge for download; http://purl.oclc.org/OCLC/PURL/DOWNLOAD.

[20] Paula Musich et al., "Cisco Lays out VPN Plans" (January 1999); http://www.zdnet.com/pcweek/stories/news/0,4153,387024,00.html.

[21] For example, Microsoft Windows NT, Windows 98, or Windows 95 with the freely available Microsoft Dial-Up Network (MSDUN) enhancement, provide for effective "Point-to-Point Tunneling Protocol" (PPTP) connections using the inherent attributes of the Microsoft operating system itself; http://www.microsoft.com.

[22] Lisa Sanger, "Caching on the Internet"; http://seamless.com/eric/cache.html.

[23] Conseil Européen pour la Recherche Nucléaire (CERN) (European Organization for Nuclear Research), "Fibre Channel Specifications"; http://www.cern.ch/HSI/fcs/spec.htm.

[24] Norman Wiseman, "INTERNET 2: Briefing Paper" (April 1999); http://www.jisc.ac.uk/pub99/internet2.html.

A case study: the power of managing knowledge in a worldwide enterprise

Ken Pratt

10.1 Introduction

This chapter looks at a case study that explores the operational and strategic benefits resulting from the application of KM principles, technologies, and tools in a large, worldwide enterprise. These are presented as a three-level model for managing knowledge and for providing insight to it, as follows:

1. Teams and communities;

2. Knowledge discovery;

3. Business transformation.

As an introduction to the driving forces behind this work, it may be helpful to understand the recent history and current organization of the large corporate subject of this study: both the BG Group and its BG Technology unit.

BG Plc is a leading international energy enterprise actively developing and supplying gas markets in 20 countries around the globe. It was formed in February 1997 as a result of the breakup of British Gas. The group has four main business units, as follows:

1. Transco, the major U.K. gas distributor;

2. BG Storage, the operator of a group of gas storage facilities in the United Kingdom;

3. BG International, responsible for international oil and gas exploration and production activities, including the development and marketing of upstream and downstream energy products;

4. Corporate Development, responsible for leading the identification and creation of new sources of shareholder value throughout the BG Group.

BG Technology is part of BG's Corporate Development unit and is responsible for providing research and technology to all BG business entities, as well as a growing cluster of external customers. BG Technology works at the leading edge of technologies related to the entire gas chain and has thousands of man-years of experience in exploration, production, transmission, distribution, storage, and energy utilization. It also sets standards for safety and environmental issues.

10.2 Problems during transformation

The need to apply KM at the heart of its operations became apparent during the transformation of BG from the nationalized U.K. gas industry into a leading international energy company because of the following key developments:

1. The need to be competitive and innovative in a cost-conscious, high-technology international market by leveraging knowledge from one part of the business to another;

2. The major reduction in staff numbers and associated skill loss meant that BG had to find ways of retaining and reusing its accumulated knowledge in the face of repositioning staff members.

Both these drivers are relevant to BG Technology as well as to BG Plc as a whole, and they are the major reasons the enterprise became active in the area of practical KM in 1997. BG's progress to date and its future plans are described in this chapter, along with experiences of achieving tangible business benefits by applying knowledge solutions to data and information problems. BG believes that knowledge is only created when it is actually used and that prejudging its potential use restricts its potential value.

10.3   Solution with first-generation KM

10.3.1   Teams and Communities

A simple, highly productive and popular starting point is to provide technology solutions and practical advice, which will enable teams and communities to share their knowledge. It is done at BG Technology with the additional goal of exploiting that knowledge outside the team, both during and beyond its lifetime, thereby greatly increasing potential benefits.

Teams and communities have different characteristics and dynamics and as a result their knowledge needs to be managed differently. BG sees a team as a group of people with common goals but not necessarily common interests—for example, a project team. Teams usually disband after a set lifetime.

Communities, on the other hand, have common interests but few if any common goals—for example, a group of chemists. They remain active for a very long time. To achieve its common goal a team has to share its knowledge among its members, but, without a common goal, there is no need for a community to share. This makes it more difficult to get community-based initiatives up and running. One basic consideration applies to both: only a few people will work effectively with a knowledge sharing system unless they benefit personally and unless minimal or zero additional effort is required. BG initiatives in first-generation KM include the following:

- The collection, storage, and delivery of knowledge for local and global teams;

- Sharing best practice case studies and ideas within dispersed communities.

10.3.1.1 Teams

There are multiple and overlapping teams throughout BG. The company's intranet KITE (Knowledge and Information to Everyone) is now available on 16,500 desktops worldwide to meet its high-level information requirements. It has been developed as a managed solution along with Lotus Notes/Domino. It is a transportable application called MaiNS (Managed Intranet Solution). It offers such features as distributed publishing, control of document authorization, audit trail, hit monitoring, and an integrated search engine.

MaiNS also solves the problem of helping a large number of distributed information publishers, while still retaining control of content and currency. It is being applied to other intranets in BG and has been made available to external companies as well. The program was awarded the Cranfield Intranet Oscar as the best intranet for 1999.

The company's intranet is structured so that a user can drill down fully through the various team hierarchies in order to gain an overview of the purpose, activities, and skills of each team and team member. Such team information is captured specifically to provide additional insights into team activities and possible interconnections. It represents the tip of the iceberg of all the knowledge produced and recorded within the organization. Other knowledge produced is for narrower objectives.

Each team within BG Technology collects this content within a team database looked upon as the team's filing cabinet. Documents placed in these databases are produced as part of the team's normal operations. This is a simple and quick-to-use application providing significant benefits to each team in terms of finding and reusing information. It also helps the overall organization to retain and restructure its knowledge base when projects are completed or teams are restructured. Users currently have full access control over who within the company can read or edit the documents in these team databases. Simple access control options are represented in check boxes: keep-it-private, publish-to-team, and publish-to-intranet. A workflow approvals process is applied whenever the last option is selected (Figure 10.1).

Team documents are easily accessible to all 16,500 BG employees, since all team databases are linked through the team's intranet pages. A log-on button to view the database via the intranet allows anyone on the network to identify himself or herself securely and then see any document he or she is entitled to see.

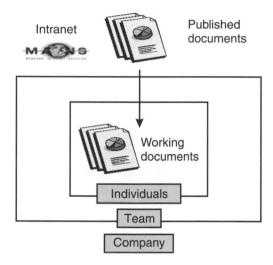

Figure 10.1 Access to published and working team documents.

Global teams As the result of a request by BG International, BG Technology created a solution to support the parent company's global teams. These teams are more difficult to support, because team members are dispersed throughout the world. They rarely meet because of great distances and the resulting extensive travel time.

A suite of tools (Figure 10.2) was developed giving these teams several key knowledge sharing components and enabling team members to

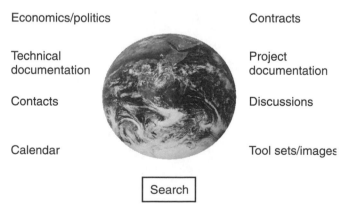

Figure 10.2 Global team knowledge sharing.

work effectively together even though separated by great distance. Most importantly, they can also work off-line.

The components available to them contain live team documentation (such as project plans and contacts) as well as common information sets, such as legal contracts, political and economic reports, and wider corporate contacts. They may also contain live input from electronic news feeds or journals such as *FT Energy*. One of the major advantages of this global team system is being able to search simultaneously across all the components available. This includes external access—for example, even while traveling in an airplane. Users are dealing with the latest information, and their colleagues have an identical set.

10.3.1.2   Communities
Communities are supported by systems from other parts of BG in the form of cross-business unit forums. These forums allow selected communities to develop and share successful procedures and case studies. They can also discuss new ideas, lessons learned, and next practice and leverage their knowledge across the entire organization.

Forums are also created for generic communities such as safety and environment, regulation and procurement throughout all BG's business units. All interaction within the forums is via a Web browser. Forum members can operate from anywhere in the company via the intranet.

10.3.2   Key first-generation lessons
The following points summarize the key lessons from BG's work on first-generation KM:

- Information ownership should be clear for each component at all levels.

- Teams and communities have very different cultural and technical knowledge sharing problems.

- A knowledge creation process that controls distributed content and feeds it easily and directly into the system is essential.

- Simple and flexible (technology) solutions are the only ones that encourage wide use, particularly by technophobes.

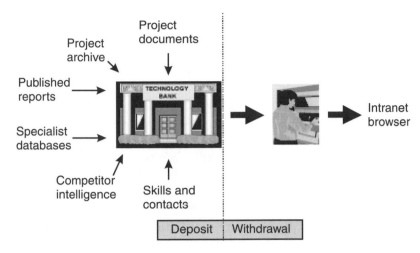

Figure 10.3 Technology knowledge bank.

10.4 Continuing solutions with second-generation KM

10.4.1 Knowledge discovery

BG Technology considers second-generation KM to be about knowledge discovery: each user is able to find out what other people in the company know. BG Technology's major work in this area has been to develop a technology knowledge bank, together with a mechanism for intelligently finding the knowledge required. The analogy of a bank has proved very powerful in communicating this concept as representing both value and security. There are several components to the technology bank (Figure 10.3). They include the following:

- ▸ *Project documents:* Items produced by project teams as part of their project work;

- ▸ *Project archive:* Past project documents;

- ▸ *Published reports:* More than 100,000 scanned and indexed pages from more than six years' proprietary research;

- ▸ *Specialist databases:* Specific technologies produced for BG Technology's customers;

‣ *Competitor intelligence:* Collated information regarding BG Technology's competitors;

‣ *Skills and contacts:* Each employee owns his or her own key skills and experience profiles.

Withdrawing knowledge from the technology bank is simple. Users need only a Web browser, a user name, and a password. Again, the bank analogy works when thinking about an ATM machine. The technology bank can be accessed in two ways: by navigating through a hierarchy or by searching. Both are accommodated through a common interface. However, the former is only really applicable if a user is withdrawing something that is known to exist and whose location is known.

The real power comes in the form of full-text, concept-based searching, and working simultaneously across the bank and other stores, such as BG's intranet, external news feeds, and targeted Web sites. This is achieved using a proprietary software product, which was selected based on the following five key criteria:

1. Its ability to search in parallel across a wide variety of information sources, with particular emphasis on Lotus Notes, scanned paper, the Web, relational databases, and native file systems;

2. Its ability to honor document-level security, particularly for Lotus Notes;

3. Its advanced search features, which go beyond basic keyword concepts and, most importantly, enable the retrieval and ranking of the documents that most closely match the meaning of the query rather than just the words;

4. Its scalability, ranging from 100 GB to 1,000 GB;

5. Its accuracy and speed.

BG Technology has worked closely with its vendor to ensure the program meets the requirements for knowledge discovery within a major international enterprise such as BG. A formal working partnership was formed between the two parties. The software is also used as the search engine on KITE, our company intranet, while both this and the technology bank application use our own proprietary user interfaces.

The power of this system is illustrated through some real-life examples, such as finding the right person to solve your problem or finding and giving a presentation to a client at a moment's notice. One of the most powerful examples emerged when the system was demonstrated to a group of BG pipeline engineers. One of them issued a challenge to search for "great crested newts." This type of newt is an endangered species and if found near an engineering site, work has to stop, with the potential to incur very large costs. Everyone was surprised with the return of two hits.

The first hit was an article from an issue of our internal BG magazine, published on the intranet, about an employee who had actually gained a newt-handling license, which legally allows him to move and rehouse newts. The second hit was a BG Technology internal report about a site visit in 1995, when newts were encountered.

This report even provided the Latin name for this newt: *Triturus Cristatus*. Also, there was some confusion regarding several other documents being returned concerning a project called Triton. This further shows the power of the search software because apparently newts are called tritons in the United States. Essentially, putting a project manager in contact with our own newt handler at a time when an ongoing pipeline project is about to be delayed could save the equivalent cost of developing the bank and purchasing the search engine in a few days.

The future success of BG will depend, in part, on the effective exploitation of its technology base. With the solutions described in this chapter, BG Technology is already demonstrating that knowledge sharing, using state-of-the-art information systems, can easily make invaluable insights available at any time to BG's business operations anywhere in the world. BG's approach to knowledge sharing can be applied much more widely, with the technology bank being seen as just one branch of a wider BG and/or partner banking network (Figure 10.4).

10.4.2 Key second-generation lessons

"Knowing who knows" is the easiest place to start: putting people in contact with knowledgeable people benefits both them and the business.

Move on to "knowing what they know" by making knowledge available across the company network so that it can be found easily.

Employ as intelligent a search engine as possible so as to get over the limitations of finding information by navigation and categorization.

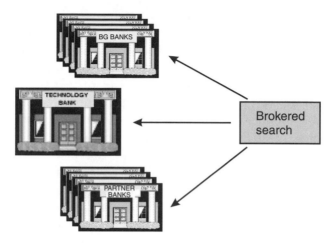

Figure 10.4   Searching across branches of the knowledge bank.

Retain the trust of information owners by ensuring that all access methods, including searching, honor their security requirements.

Never underestimate the power of serendipity; exploring knowledge you didn't know you needed to know often generates usable ideas.

10.5   What to do next: go third-generation KM

10.5.1   Business transformation

BG third-generation KM is all about "doing better things"—transforming the business rather than just increasing efficiency and moving forward in a straight line. BG Technology is now working in partnership with a team of futures consultants to bring this vision to reality.

BG Technology produced a technology and process platform that combines the approaches and technologies deployed in the work described previously. It is done with advanced content capture and management and regeneration tools, such as text mining, knowledge landscaping, and cultural change. The platform allows knowledge workers, such as strategy analysts, to exploit a company's total knowledge resources as an assist in making their decisions more accurate and timely about future business.

The approach is illustrated in Figure 10.5, with dynamic, theme knowledge bases being maintained from a multiplicity of content sources. The user interacts with this knowledge base directly or through

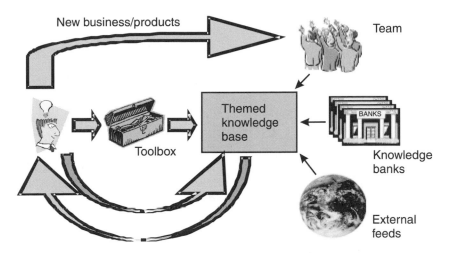

Figure 10.5   Knowledge-driven business.

a toolbox, including intelligent search, text mining (data mining with information extraction), and knowledge landscaping.

The platform will operate on a reciprocal or "give-to-get" basis, drawing further knowledge from users as they look at the contents of the knowledge base. This includes the actual and perceived values attached to any information accessed. Business transformation starts to occur when knowledge bases and operating teams function across different businesses and are prepared to work together to achieve specific business objectives.

10.6   Conclusion

To support increasing demands from the marketplace and to counteract the loss of knowledge and skills from reduced staff numbers, BG Technology embraced and successfully integrated a variety of KM practices and technologies. It learned a number of lessons in selecting and applying these technologies for its own business and is now seeking to make that learning available to other organizations. Our three-generation model has let us establish clearly our KM road map. The first two generations focus on doing things better—increasing efficiency and effectiveness—while the third is about doing better things—achieving real business innovation with partners.

KM for competitive advantage: mining diverse sources for marketing intelligence

B. J. Deering

11.1 Introduction

Any company facing competition for customers confronts the basic question, how do we anticipate and manage against initiatives intended to cut our share of the market? This is true whether the competition is a new entrant to the marketplace or a known competitor seeking greater market share. In any contested marketing environment, the organization that is best able to anticipate competitor strategies and tactics and offer real alternative value wins. The win is the retention of current valuable customers through skillful customer relationship management (CRM) and acquisition of new customers in the head-to-head marketing environment.

In the telecommunications arena CRM takes on special importance because the stakes are high. The provider selected by a customer may gain entry/loy-alty/access for a wide array of information telecommunication services, including but not limited to voice, data, video, and Internet communications. Additionally, the speed with which customer churn is possible has also accelerated, increasing the importance of having marketing intelligence immediately available for planning and implementing competitive initiatives.

Because competitor plans are never fully known ahead of time, it is essential to leverage all available information about customers' reactions to potential offers. Sometimes the information comes from the specific markets where more aggressive marketing initiatives are anticipated; sometimes the information comes from sources external to that market. In either case, effective KM requires seeking diverse data about customer and competitor activities and capitalizing on these data.

No data about a competitive situation, and customer reactions to it, will ever be perfect. Fortunately, new tools are being developed constantly that more effectively mine data and provide decision support based on that data mining. Within the past decade, modeling technology has offered significant improvements in its ability to accommodate diverse types of data, determine what is most important among those data relevant to target outcomes, and translate that learning into deci-sion-support tools.

Creating new knowledge for competitive situations requires open-ness to an enlarged array of data sources and the ability to capitalize on developments in data modeling and mining. Because of these modeling developments, information of an intuitive, qualitative nature, often the result of human intelligence gathering, can be better used in decision making. Interpretation and analysis that might otherwise lead only to directional guidance can result in more specific decision parameters. Modeling is thus better able to take data with limited numeric integrity and systematically identify and incorporate the value of these in decisions. In this case study, the prototype application of a modeling approach to KM clarifies how such openness to diverse types of information can help manage competition.

11.1.1   Ideal data to meet competitive goals
The ideal data to use for understanding and managing competition vary with both company objectives and the competitive situation being considered. In general, company goals provide focus both for specific com-

petitor and customer attributes, as well as for the level of data integrity needed to support the planning time frame. The exact competitive situation tends to determine whether data from in-market experience are available or whether more inventive sourcing has to be used.

Company goals direct requirements for data through their emphasis on immediate or longer-term application of the knowledge being built. The general goals and implied data needs are discussed in the following text.

11.1.1.1   Position for quick tactical advantage

The company seeks to develop potential response(s) for quick implementation, given alternate competitive scenarios. Data about customer response and competitor activities must focus on detailing the potential situations, with specific competitor tactics, the characteristics and identification of customers most likely to be vulnerable, and the likely impact of specific company offers within the competitive context. Data must identify a subset of customers and assess impact of varied, multiple tactics; short-term, less reliable but broad data may suffice.

11.1.1.2   Fine-tune ongoing strategy

The company goal is to enhance its ongoing marketing and service delivery programs directed at customer acquisition, retention, and value development by using new information about current or potential competitors. This goal implies data that combine current and future perspectives relevant to targeting for market share, promoting the company value proposition, and countering competitive offers.

11.1.1.3   Plan longer-term strategy

While the company continues to deliver value, the focus of this goal is to identify and plan to meet needs of the longer-term market. Such plans include forecasting and building facilities to serve a customer base years ahead and developing new products with lasting power and ability to build lifetime value. The required data tend to focus on reliability (to increase predictability) and, often, historical sources that may signal longer-term trends across time.

The specific competitive situation, in contrast to company goals, directs data requirements primarily by determining whether an in-market source exists or whether data must be invented or discovered in its entirety. Where a competitor has entered markets, its tactics and customer response in those markets can often provide a baseline for generalization, or at least a starting point, for predicting effects in a new market or where new tactics emerge. When the competitor is a new entrant, then data about it are more likely to be qualitative, often drawn from accumulation of informal sources. Examples, frequently used for competitive intelligence, are vendor and building permits, employee reports of activities, interviews among potential customers, and mystery shopping surveys.

Much of this intelligence is culled and categorized from discursive information, such as discussions with salespeople and technicians, focus groups, Web- and e-mail-based professional and customer exchanges, public media, and news and special-interest groups. This qualitative information is then categorized via content analysis for inclusion with other sources that are available directly in numeric form. While a skillful analyst can draw important conclusions from such data, these data do not lend themselves to reliable generalization into new markets and situations.

The specific competitor situation also helps determine the risk/benefit balance for improving decision making, and in this way affects data requirements. The cost of obtaining "ideal" data is more justified the greater the potential gain or loss in customer value in the competitive context. If the range of products, revenue, role in retention, or even just the segment(s) that a competitor targets suggest substantial losses, then more diverse and reliable data may be sought via primary, secondary, and analytic sources; the company will pay for more data acquisition. Equivalently, substantial competitor resources, or successes, will also tend to result in better data being sourced to improve decisions.

11.1.2 Matching real data to the ideal

Obtaining data to use for competitive advantage often means taking advantage of the most readily available sources while working to fill gaps from the ideal. This assumes that decision makers develop and share hypotheses about the impact of different drivers, allowing prioritization of potential data. Primary research, often qualitative, is helpful for establishing hypothesized drivers/relationships.

In the absence of hypotheses, prioritizing data for input is difficult. Data exploration is still possible, relying on the brute force of data-mining techniques to determine the overall descriptive or predictive power of the accumulated data. In this "kitchen sink" approach, not all techniques offer insight beyond the overall predictive power. Consequently, using techniques that are replicable and allow differentiation among inputs is recommended to help generate logical or customer-centered hypotheses about why drivers affect outcomes.

Interestingly, in many companies, the most accessible data may not be obtainable in-house. Types of data helpful for understanding competitive situations are noted in Table 11.1, along with the likelihood that they reside in-house or externally. Internal databases, while thorough in the

Table 11.1
Competitive Comparison

Type of Data	Description	Source About Own Company[a]	Source About Competitors[a]
Provider Profiles	❯ At MSA level or to zip code ❯ Historically by quarter/month.		
Value propositions	Product offers, including number, specific features/functions; pricing Service delivery quality/personnel Perceived benefits	Internal databases Internal primary research External benchmarking	External—syndicated, ad hoc, benchmarking
Brand awareness and image	Customer awareness for providers Provider attributes and evaluation	Internal primary research External syndicated External benchmarking	Internal primary research
Marketing communications	Marketing campaigns—cost, media, targets, creative content	Internal databases External syndicated	External syndicated
Sales force	Number of direct and indirect salespersons per population Compensation tactics, generating and following up inquiries	Internal databases External benchmarking	Internal primary research External benchmarking

a. Internal = inside own company; External = outside own company

Table 11.1 (continued)

Type of Data	Description	Source About Own Company[a]	Source About Competitors[a]
Customer Traits			
Locales in MSA for offers	Areas of offer; penetration rate by competitor	Internal databases	Internal primary research
	Two years history, by quarter/month		NA
Product profile and revenue	Product portfolio, revenue	Internal databases	NA at individual level; external syndicated and ad hoc for aggregate
	Product acquisitions, drops		
	Account recency/ longevity		
Demographics and firmographics	Household, business, and/or individual purchaser characteristics (e.g., number in family, number of employees, home office, economic growth in area)	Internal primary research	Internal primary research
		External syndicated, appended to database	External syndicated
Customer Shifts Among Providers	▶ To zip + 4/block level		
	▶ Two years history		
Market share	Number of current customers lost	Internal primary research	Internal primary research
	Number of potential customers lost (opportunity loss)	External syndicated	External syndicated
	Number of customers acquired/reacquired		
Share of wallet	Share of total product/service wallet lost/acquired	Internal primary research	Internal primary research
		External syndicated	External syndicated

a. Internal = inside own company; External = outside own company original data set, may not offer easy access or desired data integration or breakouts. On-Line Analytical Processing (OLAP) against corporate customer and operational databases may be restricted to the IT domain, limiting or hampering its use for KM against marketing and customer relationship objectives. Consequently, survey sources are sometimes used to recreate, at a higher level, data that reside in greater detail in-house. External sources, whether syndicated or directed toward ad hoc requirements, may provide quickest or easiest source for market-specific data.

As indicated in Table 11.1, one type of data most likely to be crucial and unavailable is details of competitor plans for a specific marketplace. Also crucial but difficult to obtain may be details of longer-term impact for corporate (or competitor) initiatives, which require systematic longitudinal data collection and ability to access these data by time. Interestingly, historical records once archived may become inaccessible for practical purposes.

11.1.3 Case study: modeling approach to build knowledge

The two U.S. markets in the case study were in the early phases of offering residential customers new alternatives for their home telephony. As with many business customers in larger metropolitan areas, who might have options among wireline, fiber, wireless, fixed wireless, cable, and satellite providers, households in the two markets were being offered at least two alternatives for local service.

The options were being offered to an increasing proportion of each city area. Within the smaller midwestern market (Dry City), with population 250,000, customers in some areas had options as early as one year before the competitive intelligence modeling began. In the other, larger, western market (Wet City), alternative service was just becoming available. Promotion for it was expected to occur soon and systematically, via localized communications and sales efforts, to alert potential new users.

The KM goal in this situation was to capitalize on the year of competition in Dry City to identify factors having the most impact on customer behaviors and to generalize that learning to Wet City as much as possible. Competitive churn, or movement of the total customer account between providers, was the outcome of most interest, but learning was also needed relevant to less marked transitions that affect revenue, such as portfolio upgrades and provider choice for multiple lines (which might have multiple providers).

This knowledge could be used in both markets to prioritize efforts, based on their likely effectiveness, and to retain and acquire valued customers via marketing, customer relationships, and product. Referring back to the role of corporate goals in defining requirements, these goals centered on fine-tuning the ongoing strategy, but also included a need to provide data-driven recommendations for positioning the organization for quick tactical advantage.

Given such a shorter-term goal, one practical approach to capitalizing on less-than-perfect data is to obtain some type of coverage in each key area, with an eye to upgrading that input as resources allow. In practice, this approach was used to develop a prototype model to predict customer behavior within the two markets. Data were assembled to represent the factors hypothesized as most critical to affecting customer response. The specific variables used for modeling, and their match against the "ideal" set, are shown in Table 11.2.

The gaps between ideal data and actual data obtained through internal groups and sources reflect the realities of accessing internal systems and competitor confidentiality about their activities. Locales for territories where offers occurred came from the internal geographic intelligence group; good at isolating neighborhoods where alternatives were available, these data were limited in terms of indicating exact timing during the year for an offer. Individual account data came primarily from the centralized corporate database and was good for history and coverage of basic products. For some of the newer products, customer drops and adds had to be specially formulated from order activity, working with the units responsible for marketing to residential customers, because the products were not yet integrated into the data warehouse.

External, syndicated sources provided two types of data not available internally, and again represented compromises between ideal and real data. For competitive advertising campaigns, the syndicated data were reliable and thorough in tracking changes weekly and monthly, but limited in detail about sub-MSA media (e.g., direct mail, door-to-door, cable ads). For customer descriptors based on neighborhood or block-level characteristics, the syndicated data offered characteristics unavailable elsewhere, but with limitations of possible outdating, given the update schedule, and inexactness of attributing a characteristic to every household in a block.

Some data in the "ideal" categories were not included in the modeling but were used to help prioritize and choose inputs for that analysis.

Table 11.2
Matching Against the Ideal

Type of Data	Description	Source About Own Company	Source About Competitors
Provider Profiles			
Value propositions	Product offers and pricing Quality of service delivery Perceived benefits	Internal records Quarterly tracking surveys Ad hoc primary research	Qualitative
Brand awareness and image	Awareness for providers Provider attributes, evaluation	Quarterly tracking surveys Ad hoc primary research	Qualitative Syndicated/U.S. total
Marketing communications	Marketing campaigns—cost, media, targets, creative content	Campaign cost, schedule, number of ads, rating points for TV and print in MSA—internal Marcom group; syndicated[a]	Campaign cost, schedule, number of ads, themes for print, television in MSA, 20 months—syndicated[a]
Sales force	Number of salespeople; tactics; compensation	Internal records	Qualitative
Customer Traits			
Locales in MSA for offers	Areas; penetration rate	Product availability by wire center geo, 3Q in year[a]	Service availability by wire center geo, 43Q in year[a]
Product profile and revenue	Product portfolio, revenue Product acquisitions, drops Account recency/ longevity	Individual household products, revenue; account history— internal records[a]	NA
Demographics and firmographics	Purchaser characteristics	Block level descriptors/ HH size, ethnicity, HH income, own/ rent, growth rate, occupations—syndicated[a]	NA

a. Input to modeling.

Table 11.2 (continued)

Type of Data	Description	Source About Own Company	Source About Competitors
Customer Shifts Among Providers			
Market share	Current and potential customer losses;winbacks, other gains	Internal records, by month[a] Share tracking surveys	NA
Share of wallet	Percentage of total wallet lost/gained	Share tracking surveys	Share tracking surveys

a. Input to modeling.

In these instances, data were not reliable enough. The competitive intelligence organization suggested likely household and neighborhood targets, based on campaigns in other markets, which led to searching for sources of household and quasieconomic descriptors relevant to the hypothesized target. Primary research suggested new products and service delivery improvements that affect satisfaction with providers, and appropriate data were sought. Surveys among customers to track market share/share of wallet suggested the importance of measuring this movement, but were not yet reliable enough at the specific market level to be included

An overview of the competitive time frame, as well as data inputs (Table 11.3), clarifies that some information tracked changes across almost two years, while other inputs marked single or scattered nonrecurring events. One of the challenges of managing such data is marrying analyses that are sensitive to potential time-based effects with analyses appropriate to data where no trends or lags can be ascertained.

11.1.4 Modeling technology to capitalize on diverse data

Several modeling technologies offer the ability to determine the explanatory power of diverse and less-than-perfect data points. These data-mining techniques can generate predictions in the absence of hypotheses, although, as noted, hypotheses ease the selection of inputs and interpretation of results. Such methods include machine learning, such as neural networks, decision trees, and genetic algorithms. Classification tree analysis was used in the case study, for its ability to analyze dependencies among data while being open to a wide array of potential driver-outcome

Table 11.3
Overview of Modeling Residential Retention with Telephony Competition

Time Period for Modeling: Customer churn and product choices across nine months (test period)

Customers Analyzed: Current customers selected at random in each city preceding the test period.

Modeling Approach

History, going forward. Among customers present at the start of the test period, who churns to the competitor, who stays, what are they like? (Prospective cohort analysis.) This is the basic analytic approach used.

Disconnect going backward. Among customers who disconnected, what are they like compared to a group who stayed? (Retrospective case-control analysis.) This framework, based on selecting churned customers and matching them to others, was used to generate hypotheses about key drivers.

Potential Drivers

▶ Customer account history for one year preceding the test period. (19 products/month)

▶ Customer demographics immediately preceding the test period. (20 descriptors)

▶ Product offers and competitive alternative availability for each customer, as of end of test period.

▶ Advertising across test period. (40 inputs/month-media × campaigns × two companies)

relationships [1]. Although extending across almost a two-year period, these data were not appropriate for traditional methods, such as time series and dynamic regression, that usually rely on several years of historical data.

In general, classification trees search for the best predictor by systematically identifying which input variable best differentiates individuals on the outcome or dependent variable (i.e., customers who do or do not churn). Once a variable has been selected, the tree looks for the next best predictor given that the effect of the preceding inputs has been taken into account. Trees can vary in the criterion for improved prediction that determines when enough variables have entered (the tree stops growing), but they share the general advantage of condensing large data sets into a relatively small number of prediction rules. Advantages of tree analysis will be demonstrated in examples from the case study.

In addition to using modeling techniques with the flexibility to accept diverse data and relationships, developing knowledge about the competitive scenarios also benefited from previous modeling. This work had established an efficient way to look at how customers make transitions between states or positions represented by the product portfolio and other aspects of changing product acquisitions and drops. Because of this transition-based modeling, marketplace drivers could be weighed against a limited number of customer states, including churn to competitors. Without the foundation work to estimate conditional transition intensities, based on millions of historical data points (customer product adds and drops across two years), the trees would have been less efficient or effective in identifying key drivers.

11.1.5 Results for modeling in competitive contexts

Results from the case study demonstrated that very diverse, less-than-perfect data can be combined via modeling to improve the understanding and prediction of competitive impact. Using the modeling algorithm, customers were separated into groups whose churn likelihood differs fourfold: One group went to the competitor at four times the rate of another. A difference in probability of competitive loss for subsets was found for customers who differ in characteristics selected as most important by the classification tree. Each city had a unique effect in itself, independent of the other data included in the model.

As expected, the churn rate is higher in Dry City, where competition has been available longer. Beginning with a total 5,820 customers, of whom 3.7 percent had competitively disconnected; among Dry City customers (2,992 of the total), the churn rate was 6.7 percent, compared with only 0.6 percent in the other market. Beyond that, looking at drivers within each city, it was not surprising, and somewhat of a reality check on the modeling technology, that the availability of a specific competitive opportunity is the most important driver for churn. Disconnects are higher in Company B territory (8.5% versus 2.5% out of its territory—DryCity).

Secondary to competitor territory came an indicator of the customer's portfolio "lifestage" (account age), offers for several specific products, a single advertising input (monthly cost for print ads), and one economic indicator at the block level (population growth, year over year). More specifically we learned the following:

- Seventeen percent of the oldest accounts defect, versus 6% of youngest accounts;

- Six percent of homes not subscribing to Product X defect, versus less than 1% of homes with it;

▸ Defection is lower among Product W and Product V subscribers;

▸ Population growth (block level) areas have lower defection rates.

It was found that a small number of drivers best captured all the predictive information from the input 100+ variables. The effects of other variables, to the extent they have any impact, were captured through their relationships with the other variables; their effects flow through the other variables.

Effective development of knowledge also recognizes that the meaning and import of the same facts and data may vary with the situation being assessed. In the competitive situations for the two markets, the same potential driver may have different overall impact in each city. An example was where retention is greatest (10% disconnects) at both a moderately high level and at the lowest level of advertising by Company A.

There is not a simple increase in retention for its customers as Company A boosts its advertising. Similarly, data-mining techniques recognize that the effect of one driver may depend on another. Advertising impact for Company A, for instance, varied with the level of advertising by Company B. The specific breakpoints separating advertising by levels of impact are determined by the modeling, to maximize effect on disconnects, and may not correspond to levels usually used for media buys.

While considering the relative impact of variables on churn to alternate providers, it was also important to confirm that the data mining elicited effects truly connected to competitive scenarios, not to customer movement in general. Customers move constantly; complete turnover for an area every five years, on average, is common for many U.S. metropolitan areas. How can data mining help assure that key variables are not just tapping into ongoing progressions in customers' lives that do not reflect competitive presence? One approach was to analyze the same potential drivers against customer churn that is not for competitive reasons and compare resultant predictors and their weights in the competitive and noncompetitive instances.

Only one household characteristic emerged as important for predicting both competitive and noncompetitive movement: account age. Otherwise, the variables linked to competitive disconnects do not surface, while new ones do, including marital status and portfolio stability (time since last change). In brief, top drivers for competitive and noncompetitive churn differ; the modeling successfully focuses on factors unique to competitive scenarios. Also confirming successful distinction by the modeling was the fact that noncompetitive disconnects are not elevated in the territory for competitive offers.

11.2   Solutions for decision support

As demonstrated in the case study, modeling in two competitive markets provided its immediate and longer-term informational results. The modeling quantified the effect of both selected company product offers and of competitive alternatives on customer retention. It identified customer characteristics associated with churn probability, given the selected offers and competitor alternatives. Finally, it developed a scoring algorithm to categorize customers according to their susceptibility to competitive offers.

In providing these outcomes, the modeling also accomplished the data management goal of assessing the predictive value of new data sources, by incorporating individual and aggregate customer data. The data-mining approach successfully integrated measures at the individual customer level with indicators tied to citywide and sub-MSA geographic areas.

For business decisions, the modeling provided fundamental insight for several marketing and resource allocation applications, as follows:

- More vulnerable consumers can be identified and targeted effectively using a combination of data sources, before and during head-to-head competition.

- Retention value of specific product offers can be estimated. Churn and retention can be supplemented by the associated lifetime value of retained customers to guide decisions about cost effectiveness of deploying new products.

- Company marketing communications can increase their impact by planning media schedules that recognize tradeoffs among company campaigns, and interaction with competitor campaigns, in terms of effect on customers' behavior.

- Forecasting basic requirements for company facilities can become more accurate by incorporating probable customer transitions, rolling up the modeled information about household churn and product acquisitions and drops to the city level. The modeling was used to enhance an earlier tree-based forecasting [2] methodology.

Decision support software tools were not provided as part of the data-mining output but would be essential for successful ongoing use of the modeling capabilities. In general, decision makers requested desktop tools that would provide them with not only on-line inquiry capability but also the ability to simulate outcomes from variations in the key drivers identified via the modeling. This simulation capability has been provided previously via a variety of decision analysis and display options (e.g., ITHINK, Statistica, Analytika) [3].

Finally, both the data inputs and modeling algorithms are candidates for systematization through the corporate data warehouse. The warehouse is a centralized repository for data about customers, and is also a foundation for the CRM system, which can score individuals for targeting, managing inbound calls, and offering products. In the case study modeling, only the billing input was pulled directly from the centralized database; the other inputs will need to be incorporated in that base before the model can be used in its entirety.

To improve the CRM system by integrating modeling into it, another requirement would be the ability to efficiently score the entire customer base using the scoring algorithm. This capability did exist at the end of the project, reflecting an in-house modeling environment that updates scoring algorithms on sampled customers and then connects to the warehouse via batch processing. Plans exist to move toward real time rather than batch updating.

11.2.1 New directions and products

AMR Research predicts that growth in the CRM market will exceed 40% per year over the next several years. That phenomenal expectation helps explain why enterprise resource planning (ERP) firms, whose software handles back-office functions, have reached out to the front office through aggressive acquisitions or by developing their own tools. For example, PeopleSoft purchased call center Vantive; SAP plans a front-office capability; and Oracle is already marketing an e-business suite, which adds front-office CRM capability to its back-office functionality.

Analytical CRM is a powerful tool, although, surprisingly, it is used by only about half of CRM implementers, according to the META Group. Although significant challenges remain in integrating data from disparate sources into one data warehouse, analytical CRM provides the greatest value when it combines front- and back-office data, such as customer revenues, to guide marketing and other planning efforts. In fact, both the Gartner Group and AMR believe that CRM companies lacking a back-office component will significantly limit their client base in future years.

In addition to a comprehensive data warehouse, the other key ingredient is an analytical technique such as OLAP, which produces analyses requested by the user, or data mining, which searches for patterns in data that the user may not have suspected. The results of those analyses determine which business rules are triggered, most often implementing a market campaign but sometimes modifying workflow or other business process. The nature of marketing has changed dramatically in the past few years, in terms of both timing and focus [4].

IBM's DecisionEdge for relationship marketing enables organizations to identify, acquire, develop, and retain profitable customers. The business intelligence software is designed for specific industries to identify which prospects would make the best customers, which customers are good prospects for additional products and services, and which customers may be at risk for leaving. It also features a campaign management capability to manage and track highly targeted marketing campaigns and ongoing interactions with large volumes of customers and prospects.

DecisionEdge employs analysis and predictive modeling techniques that allow customer segmentation, analysis, and scoring valuable data derived from transaction systems, Web sites, operational systems, and external sources. That enables you to analyze events and predict customer behavior with a much greater level of accuracy, injecting the results of the analysis into the marketing relationship you establish with individual customers in near real time [5].

CoVia (www.covia.com) is providing software to develop corporate portals for specific job functions. InfoPortal Sales Edition and Marketing Editions (each starting at $225,000) channel pertinent business information and offer specific features to help close deals faster and retain and upsell customers. Sales Edition users start with a virtual sales desk catered to the account manager's needs, including data, documents, tasks, discussions, and market news feeds. Account managers can also link their virtual sales desk to the portal, a plus for the business traveler who gains Web access, making the tool as effective on the road as at the office. Sales Edition features the ability to deploy ProspectNets, called one-to-one portals or private extranets. ProspectNets are offered to qualified prospects to facilitate collaboration through a long sales cycle. Within the software, parties can go through sales presentations and collateral, work on RFPs, and even negotiate a final contract [6].

With Sybase PowerDesigner business analysts, designers, database administrators, developers, and project managers have access to a single tool, which allows them to take advantage of both object-modeling and data-modeling techniques with full repository capabilities. The rapid application development design tool enables designers and developers to improve productivity throughout the development cycle, from analysis and design through database schema generation and business object generation. PowerDesigner features improved Unified Modeling Language (UML), class diagram modeling, and an enhanced repository for refined enterprise modeling. Multiple users can simultaneously store and share design information [7].

11.3 Conclusion

The case study results demonstrate that modeling can be used to create effective marketing intelligence for use in competitive situations. It confirms that this intelligence can be developed in situations where available data are less than perfect in their comprehensiveness and (statistical) reliability. Decision makers can be provided with directional information for current and emerging situations by managing the available information to capitalize on its combined predictive power. Modeling improved on intelligence that was based on only one type of data in earlier efforts, especially by providing guidance early in competitor entry.

Based on the case study results, decision makers facing competitive situations should be encouraged to welcome and consider any type of data that might be related to understanding customer and competitor activities. In fact, every type of data input in the modeling contributed, through some specific variables, to understanding drivers for churn. They should assess the value of using such diverse data against the appropriate in-market criteria, including measuring the predictive power of these data via data mining.

Partially because data mining is relatively low cost in the context of marketing and IT budgets, decision makers should also experiment with a wide range of approaches, expanding on traditional methodologies that restrict potential inputs or predetermine relationships. Modeling costs only a fraction of a small-scale marketing campaign and can provide guidance for such campaigns. It can also estimate the payoff of the considerably larger cost of capitalizing on new knowledge from modeling by supporting the software and/or systematization required for ongoing decision support.

As Harry Kolar, Director, Business Intelligence Strategies, of IBM said, "Companies need data to become and to remain competitive. You have to be extremely responsive to the market. At IBM we want to leverage every piece of data we can get our hands on. Everything is incorporated—anywhere a customer interacts with us, we capture it. It can be a call into a call center or an 800 number; it can be a service-related issue or a purchase. The key is to tie all those together in a unified system so you can treat your customers properly and honor their preferences." [8]

To maximize the value of modeling as a tool for knowledge creation, its sponsors within an organization need to assure that development and application efforts, like the case study, contribute to the accumulation of business intelligence. This requires that each effort be planned against a particular marketing or resource allocation situation, however recurrent. The true marker for modeling success is not lift attributed to it in one specific campaign, but rather the cumulative contribution of modeling to helping the company achieve its goals.

References

[1]   L. Brieman, J. Friedman, R. Olshen, and C. Stone, *Classification and Regression Trees* Wadsworth publishing. /OR/L.A., Jr., 1996. Using causal knowledge to learn more useful decision rules from data. Chapter 2 in D. Fisher and H-J Lenz (Eds), *Learning from Data: Artificial Intelligence and Statistics* V.Springer-Verlag, New York.

[2]   L. A. Cox, Jr., *Learning Improved Demand Forecasts or Telecommunications Products from Cross-Sectional Data* (Cox Associates, Denver, CO: 1998).

[3]   D. Buede, "Decision Analysis Software Survey: Aiding Insight IV," *ORMS Today* (August 1998): 56–64.

[4]   "Analytical CRM: Capturing Data to Cater to Customers," *KMWorld* (January 15, 2001).

[5]   "KM Moving up to Center Stage," *KMWorld* (March 1, 2000).

[6]   Ibid.

[7] "Sybase Rolls out Repository with Object and Data Modeling Tool," *KMWorld* (October 10, 2000).

[8] "Count on It," *The Industry Standard* (March 26, 2001).

Acknowledgments

The author thanks several individuals for their support, contributions, and insightful comments: Dean Dugan, Renee Karson, William Stewart, Dr. Tony Cox, and Dr. Jay Gillette.

B. J. Deering

Contents

Building knowledge communities with webs of connections

Barbara Weaver Smith

12.1 Background

A knowledge community is a web of connections among people with a common interest and a desire to learn. Knowledge communities connect people who know with people who want to know; collectively, the community knows more than each member knows individually. Members of a knowledge community do not merely exchange information; through dialog, they create new knowledge, knowledge that organizations are learning to leverage for innovation in products, processes, customer services, and trade.

Knowledge communities are natural human constructs. Each of us belongs to many knowledge communities—clubs, professional associations, faith institutions, and other social networks. But in the networked economy, corporations such as edmunds.com are deliberately employing

201

new technology capabilities to create knowledge communities with their customers, suppliers, trading partners, and competitors. Although these knowledge communities are enabled by the speed and accessibility of communications and by new tools for data and information management, they are nonetheless primarily about human interaction.

Knowledge communities are not new. "As in the old practice of storytelling, people re-experience an event together and learn its meaning collectively" [1]. Storytelling has been used on an informal basis, around the water cooler and in staff meetings, and on a formal basis, published histories and memorial awards, for many years. Most of a Web site, www.stevedenning.com, is dedicated to storytelling.

This chapter explores two particular ways in which knowledge communities are evolving in the networked economy. One evolution is "virtual" participation through Internet connections rather than face-to-face encounters. The second is the strategic business practice of building knowledge communities on purpose. The materials used in storytelling about a particular company aspect or one of its "characters" can be used in both ways. My own experience includes the traditional as well as the new forms of knowledge communities.

As a former English professor, I have belonged to academic knowledge circles in classrooms, professional associations, conferences, brown-bag lunches, and break-room conversations. As the chief executive of a nonprofit cultural organization, I struggled with the challenges of engaging employees, board members, constituents, and supporters in sustained, purposeful conversation to advance the organization's mission and programs. Today, as the founding owner of a professional services firm, I participate actively in several on-line knowledge communities and serve as the convening host/facilitator of "Talking Culture, Talking Knowledge," [2] an international virtual community whose members practice KM in diverse fields, including education, business consulting, banking, technology, and philanthropy. Through these experiences I have come to regard knowledge communities both as fragile, ephemeral associations that can dissolve overnight and as powerful, enabling associations whose learning benefits far exceed any formal educational programs I have known.

I categorize knowledge communities at three levels of increasing value: communities of interest, sometimes known as peer to peer (P2P); communities of practice; and communities of exchange. These communities differ in purpose, and therefore in depth and breadth, from a short-term association among random customers to a high-powered, high stakes sustained association among competitors. They derive their power, and their business potential, from the strength of the shared interest and the strategic management of their communal resources.

12.1.1 Communities of interest

Easy access to the Internet has spawned hundreds of thousands of on-line communities populated by individuals who share a common interest. List-servs, chat rooms, and bulletin boards provide virtual spaces where people gather to exchange information about any interest, from training dogs or collecting dolls to political rants and eliminating world hunger. Low-cost and no-cost technology platforms support these groups, the largest being eGroups [3], recently acquired by Yahoo! In April 2000, eGroups' e-mail group service had more than 14 million active members participating in over 600,000 e-mail groups and exchanging over 2 billion e-mail messages per month in multiple languages. eGroups is a free service that includes an on-line calendar, databases, directories, a mechanism for option polls among members, and a Web-based exchange in addition to e-mail distribution. Most of the on-line communities are social networks, not commercial ones.

For commercial purposes, a minimal version of the knowledge community, what I call a community of interests, takes the form of an on-line forum for customer support. A typical on-line help desk is the "Webnews" discussion boards established by AT&T WorldNet Internet service. WorldNet employees host and monitor hundreds of discussions, each focused on a specific customer problem or question. But WorldNet staff do not provide all of the help. Customers who visit the on-line discussion contribute their own knowledge and engage in mutual problem solving. For example, I struggled to configure a new handheld computer running the WindowsCE operating system, unable to make it communicate with my WorldNet e-mail account. When I posted my problem to the Webnews discussion about "configuring Windows CE devices," I learned that other people had the same problem and that there was no quick fix.

Each hardware device had its own quirky system, and configuration required unique kinds of tweaking. WorldNet staff offered "solutions" that did not work for me, but I received advice from many other customers, not only through replies on the discussion board but also through personal e-mails and offers to walk me through a solution over the phone. WorldNet customers referred me to Web sites, sent lines of programming code, and commiserated. For a couple of weeks, until my problem was solved, I "belonged" to this community of interest—people who discovered the same technology problem that I had and who were eager to share their hard-won new knowledge with others. Although the WorldNet staff itself did not solve my problem, the on-line community did. At the same time, WorldNet personnel were learning about bugs in their system, presenting their corporation as a dedicated service provider, and averting a horde of disgruntled customers.

Napster is probably the best-known example of P2P computing. Napster enabled 40 million users to access any music files wanted in a directory on your hard drive that you designate as available to Napster. Aimster [4] is another P2P application, with two differences. First, it's not aimed at any particular type of file. Second, rather than opening up my desktop directory to millions of strangers, it only makes it available to people on an AOL instant messaging "buddy list."

This does to document development what the Web did to document publishing. Without having to do any additional work, buddies can access the documents you're working on or relying on. So, imagine that you are part of the new project to decide where in Europe we'll open our next office. You set up a folder on your desktop and tell your P2P DM app to make it available to the other people in the project. You set up subfolders as well. Maybe you tell your P2P app that a particular folder should only be visible to some subset of your project buddies. As you add documents that you want to share (an article on changes to the tax law in Belgium, links to Web sites about the livability of Dutch cities) and documents you are working on (initial thoughts about why Antwerp is currently your favored city), the P2P app does some document management work: it indexes them, notes new versions, tracks access, builds a browsable portal, notices similarities to other projects underway across the enterprise, and so on. It does this without intruding one whit on your work.

It's not clear to me whether P2P document management will come from the old line document management companies or from the new P2P application vendors such as groove.net. Vendors have consistently underestimated the difficulty of building robust document management apps, so it may be hard for a hip-'n'-hot P2P company to succeed, whereas it wouldn't be hard for a project or document management company to add instant messaging and P2P capabilities. On the other hand, the document management companies will be tempted to see P2P as a way to sneak in the sort of over-kill megatonnage that has kept their products off of hundreds of millions of desktops in the first place. Maybe some document management and P2P vendors will combine forces. But, one way or another, P2P will be the future of document management.

12.1.2 What does it do for Edmunds?

In 1966, a company called Edmunds launched what became a very successful publishing business, selling consumer information in the form of annual guides to buying and selling new or used cars and trucks. In 1994, however, at the dawn of the Internet, Edmunds's management made a remarkable decision—to offer its proprietary information from a Web site at no cost to consumers. The company provided free information, not to help customers buy Edmunds's products but to help their customers buy and sell motor vehicles in the automotive marketplace. In 1996, the company changed its name to edmunds.com, fully embracing a new business model. Whereas in prior years I had purchased Edmunds's auto guides whenever I wanted to buy or sell a car, now I could log on to edmunds.com and get the same information free.

Not only does edmunds.com post consumer information compiled by its staff, it also launched Edmunds Town Hall, an on-line gathering space where people converse about buying and selling cars, maintaining cars, auto safety, motorsports, mechanics, and a host of other industry and consumer issues. The Town Hall features frequent live chats with automotive and motorsports experts and celebrities. Edmunds.com asks on-line visitors for feedback, and proud buyers and sellers post public messages to brag about their deal. They recommend the Edmunds Web site to family and friends, and the audience grows.

Sounds like a great service for consumers—but what did it do for Edmunds?

Through its bold leap into the connected economy, edmunds.com captured the attention and participation of 1.3 million unique visitors a month, according to recent counts. As a result, other business partners and affiliates pay Edmunds a premium for the opportunity to reach the auto-buying public at edmunds.com, offering insurance, accessories, auto and financing services, and aftermarket parts for sale to this vast market. Although edmunds.com still publishes its automotive guides, its corporate value is not primarily the profit on book sales but the aggregate value of an automotive knowledge community.

12.1.3   Accelerating business

Creating an on-line community about products and services can be a powerful means of accelerating business innovation. Help-desk personnel encounter new problems every day; they seldom know all the answers or even all the questions. Customers help to grow corporate knowledge, which, if well managed, leads to continued improvement. Further, communities of interest attract the hackers and tinkerers who force technology into new applications. Learning to listen to them can reveal new product and service ideas and new markets.

A manufacturer of surgical equipment learned through its message board that a surgeon was taking scalpels to a machine shop to have them reshaped for a new surgical procedure. Because the help-desk staff had a system to share such knowledge with product engineers, the discovery led to the invention of a new product line. Extracting value from these interchanges, however, requires a comprehensive KM approach, ranging from the supporting technology to the flow of information from help desk to engineering, product development, purchasing, manufacturing, marketing, and sales.

In the field of KM, the best-known community of interest gathers at the @brint.com Web site (www.brint.com), billed as a business and technology knowledge portal and a global community network. Brint's founder, Yogesh Malholtra, has combined a comprehensive array of on-line business and technology resources with an active series of discussion boards. @Brint intends to be the one-stop on-line source of business and technology news. Most of the purportedly millions of people who log on to @Brint use the service purely as a research tool for links to reports, books, Web sites, articles, and other media. This practice does not constitute a "community," because participants interact with information, not with other people.

There is, however, a community of interest engaged in @Brint's on-line forums. There any member may post a topic for discussion in hopes of generating interest, advice, and resources from others. The on-line discussion is a kind of filter through which people locate others who share their professional interests and business questions. With luck, they get more pertinent and contextual advice and links to more applicable resources than a simple search of the site would offer. Participants are grappling with specific tasks, projects, and opportunities in their own work; tapping into a global information community is faster and more reliable than merely locating documents. For example, in the @Brint on-line discussion called Knowledge Management Think Tank, a member from the Netherlands started a topic about communities and yellow pages. His request was this: I am currently doing research on communities and yellow pages. I'd like some comments, feedback, consideration, and ideas for other sources of information. He elaborated his thinking and his purposes. Over six weeks time, the conversation grew to encompass 25 thoughtful messages among six participants from the United States, Canada, Israel, and India. Together, they constitute a community of interest, having come together for discussion of an important issue in their work and research responsibilities. They will disperse whenever they believe they have extracted the full value of their communication, but many will continue to participate in similar discussions on an infinite variety of topics related to their business.

12.1.4 Communities of practice

A distinctive limitation of the community of interest is that members engage in common learning and exploration but not in common work. Typically they do not know each other well beyond the confines of the immediate discussion. To whom do you turn regularly for trusted advice? Who helps you increase your capability to do your own job? To whom are you acting as a mentor, coach, or learning partner? Chances are those people are members, with you, of a Community of Practice (CoP).

Communities of practice are purposeful knowledge communities that cut across formal boundaries within and between organizations. They are more durable than communities of interest, because together members are constructing the knowledge base of their profession or trade while they are doing work. CoP members may be coworkers, but membership often extends far beyond the workplace. According to Etienne Wenger, author of the most comprehensive studies of CoPs, a community of practice defines itself by its purpose, its functions, and its production of resources [5].

Wenger explains, "We frequently say that people are an organization's most important resource. Yet we seldom understand this truism in terms of the communities through which individuals develop and share the capacity to create and use knowledge. Even when people work for large organizations, they learn through their participation in more specific communities made up of people with whom they interact on a regular basis. These communities of practice are mostly informal and distinct from organizational units. However, they are a company's most versatile and dynamic knowledge resource and form the basis of an organization's ability to know and learn." [6]

A strong community of practice fulfills many roles of a guild, inculcating newer members into professional values, practices, vocabulary, tacit knowledge, and rituals. CoPs create and hold in trust an organization's most significant, useful, and applicable knowledge.

12.2 Solutions

A community of practice benefits from a diverse membership in terms of culture, nationality, gender, age, experience, cognitive style, and personality. Although people have always reached beyond their immediate boundaries for new ideas, the networked world allows more people to participate, more frequently, at less cost. The international scientific community maintained communities of practice through travel, correspondence, professional journals, and eventually telephone calls, but these are expensive means of contact that constrained the number and frequency of knowledge exchanges. The global Web offers unprecedented speed, cost savings, and diversity. For that reason, CoPs may exist partly or wholly in virtual workspace.

Many corporations now work deliberately to build communities of practice among their employees. Corporate directories in the form of "yellow pages," databases of lessons learned and best practices, on-line discussion groups, and formal or informal agreements for people to be "on call" to one another may support the development of new CoPs.

Chris Collison [7] spearheaded a series of KM initiatives to create CoPs at British Petroleum. BP's merger with Amoco posed new challenges for integrating knowledge and practice from two global companies. So Collison invented "Connect," a program designed to prompt "ten-minute phone calls and e-mail help requests" among employees of BP Amoco. By 1999, more than 12,000 people had voluntarily designed and published a "Connect" home page to the corporate intranet. Organized around key business questions, the evolving database of employee skills, experiences, and connections links people with a question to people who may have an answer.

By publishing a Connect page, employees signal their willingness to assist other BP Amoco staff across divisional and global boundaries. Employees search the home pages by means of key questions such as "who knows x?" or "who has done y?" Static documents stored in company databases contain links to their authors' Connect page, offering any inquirer the opportunity to relate the report to the deeper experience and practice of those who produced it. Collison believes, "As the oil industry continues to adapt to harsh market conditions—and mergers and acquisitions abound—the ability to harness the intellectual capacity of a rapidly evolving work force will be a key competitive advantage." [7]

12.2.1 Sharing knowledge

The World Bank continuously refines its global knowledge sharing strategy, defined as "sharing knowledge to fight poverty." The Bank has instituted thematic communities of practice, supported by staff members whose role is to gather and share knowledge from one country that can be applied in another part of the world. The Bank's practice is to share stories, internally and externally, about the value of communities of practice. Here is one example from the Bank's Internet site [8]: July 27, 1999, Tirana, Albania. A staff member, advising the Albanian Ministry of Education, had a problem. The Pedagogical Institute had just asked him for examples of educational strategy statements from other countries—and how stakeholders were involved in their preparation. And it wanted the responses immediately, since they were to be a key input for a meeting with the minister.

He e-mailed the Education Advisory Service, which immediately sent examples of education strategies for India, Georgia, Philippines, Poland, and New Zealand—as well as surveys of such strategies for Asia and other Eastern European countries. The next day it sent strategies for Yemen and Guyana. A day after that, still a day before the meeting with the minister, a member of the education thematic community added examples from the United Kingdom, France, Ireland, Germany, Portugal, Netherlands, Spain, and Iceland.

The staff member armed the Institute with exactly the kind of material it had requested—and discussed how the knowledge might apply to Albania. With the request likely to recur, the material has been edited for reuse and entered into the knowledge base so that staff can tap the material directly.

For every successful corporate initiative to create knowledge communities, probably 100 attempts have failed, most often because they emphasize tools instead of people. If a new intranet, database, or communication system is perceived to increase workload rather than enable better work, people will resist or circumvent that system. Communities of practice arise spontaneously through unpredictable Webs of random interactions, introductions, referrals, and connections. Whereas a community of interest may serve short-term, occasional, or avocational needs, communities of practice are devoted to serious professional development. What holds them together is their relevance to members' recurring needs for information, knowledge, learning, and understanding.

They thrive on reciprocity and mutual negotiation of ground rules, and they go underground in the face of command and control. While they cannot be "managed" too tightly, CoPs can be encouraged, and they will benefit from management support in the form of learning opportunities, resources, recognition, encouragement, and reward.

12.2.2 Communities of exchange

Communities of practice are more professional than commercial. Although their benefits accrue to commercial enterprise, their members may have stronger loyalties to their professional practice than to their employer. A third type of knowledge community—what I call a community of exchange—deliberately serves commercial exchanges.

Knowledge communities have always gathered around markets— think of the agora, the bazaar, the trading post, and the seaport. Information and knowledge travel the timeworn paths of commerce. But in the networked economy, industries are inventing new trading networks through which they may choose to share their most sacrosanct knowledge with suppliers, competitors, and customers. KM practice and supporting technologies open new doors for trading networks that enable participants in a comprehensive value chain to reduce costs, increase reliability, and gain marketplace advantages.

Commerce One [9] defines itself as a "Global Trading Net," building global Web-enabled marketplaces that support "trading with anyone, anywhere, any time." The company was founded in 1994, became Commerce One in 1997, went public in 1999, and now employs 3,500 employees around the world in association with 1,400 service providers for technology, strategy, design, marketing, and other core business services. Commerce One's global trading Web aggregates trading networks in multiple industries. Dee Hock, founder of the VISA credit card network, calls this model "co-opetition"—cooperation among competitors.

Mark Hoffman, CEO of Commerce One, expresses this corporate vision: Businesses will communicate, interact, and transact with each other as never before. Companies within trading communities will operate as if they are each other's internal departments. The future of electronic commerce will be interactive, dynamic, and real time—within the enterprise and between enterprises.

12.3 What to do next

Companies now have an opportunity to revolutionize both how they procure goods and how they transact and interact with their trading community. This is a vision not only of revolutionizing procurement within the four walls of an enterprise, but also extending the solution beyond the enterprise, to interact electronically with suppliers, customers, and distributors. In short, it is a vision of completely integrated, end-to-end electronic commerce solutions, which tie corporate intranets and extranets together. The age of the integrated supply chain—delivering benefits for buying and supplying organizations—is here [10].

Among Commerce One's market networks is Trade-Ranger [11], whose founding partners include Royal Dutch/Shell, BP Amoco, Conoco, Dow Chemical, Equilon Enterprises, Mitsubishi Corporation, Motiva Enterprises, Occidental Petroleum, Phillips Petroleum, Repsol YPF, Statoil, Tosco, TotalFinaElf, and Unocal. According to Commerce One, the exchange will enable buyers and sellers to achieve significant savings in time and money by simplifying transaction processes while providing broad access to larger numbers of customers. Membership is available to all companies, buyers and sellers, in the energy and petrochemical community and provides the ability to trade goods and services in a secure, independent, and open marketplace.

Covisint is a new Internet exchange for automakers and their suppliers, founded in February 2000 by the former Big Three Detroit automakers, General Motors, Ford, and DaimlerChrysler AG. The purpose is for members to transact business faster and cheaper than they have ever done before, improving quality and reducing costs in automotive products. The network's value will derive from sharing formerly proprietary knowledge in order to integrate supply with demand. Covisint's enormous challenge is to build sufficient trust within the network so that all members will realize benefits from their participation.

Since the plan was announced, reporters have chronicled FTC concerns that collusion among the automakers would squeeze suppliers. Many suppliers—large and small—express trepidation about exposing themselves in this network. Nevertheless, the value proposition has attracted more than 250 customers who participate in the virtual on-line trading community [12].

As these examples illustrate, communities of trade are revolutionizing business models and practice on a global scale.

12.4 Conclusion

12.4.1 Building successful knowledge communities

Successful business practice in the networked economy depends on what people know, how fast they can learn, and how much and how often they will share knowledge with other stakeholders in the enterprise. Today's business depends on customer knowledge, process knowledge, product knowledge, and tacit knowledge of how to get things done. It requires a robust corporate memory, accessible to everyone just when they need to know, so that prior experience, innovation, solutions, tactics, and strategies lead to continuous learning and improvement rather than being invented anew on each new occasion. Technology alone cannot enable this kind of organizational knowledge, for it is more than data and documents—it is the collective talent, skill, and experience of the stakeholders operating in a culture of trust and sharing.

Trust is the primary requisite for a thriving knowledge community. In a corporate culture where closely held knowledge and expertise equates to power, sharing knowledge freely is a risky business that turns traditional practice on its ear.

A culture of mutual trust requires shared beliefs about failure, risk, and reward. Fear of failure and criticism is anathema to a knowledge community. Strong knowledge communities seek out their failures, analyze them, learn from them, and use their experience to improve. Strong knowledge communities encourage strategic risk-taking and reward sharing in tangible and intangible ways.

When corporate knowledge communities extend into the customer base, a strategy of "launch, listen, and learn" may be critical. Releasing products or services in a not-yet-perfect mode allows customers to codesign the next iteration, but this strategy requires a high level of communication and responsiveness.

Mergers and acquisitions threaten knowledge communities. The significant players who contribute the most knowledge to the system may not be apparent in organizational charts or recognized by job titles. CoP members may feel more loyalty to their practice than to their employer.

In each of the merging organizations, knowledge communities have unique methods, practices, and systems. Preserving and increasing a new organization's intellectual capital requires deliberate attention to supporting and integrating knowledge communities.

When CoPs extend throughout an industry, crossing the lines between and among competitive corporations, they raise many issues of corporate policy. What is appropriate for employees of one company to share with employees of another? Software engineers, for example, notoriously rely on communities of practice to help in developing new applications. Technologies are invented, refined, debugged, and revised only through the constant tinkering of groups of innovators with long tentacles into their communities of practice. A script, a line of code, and a thousand small solutions from a hundred practitioners are requisite for successful inventions of new technologies.

Industry standards emerge only from sharing knowledge and information across competitive lines. Most of this essential work is accomplished through communities of practice long before deliberate corporate intervention sets the parameters for information exchange. Only by practicing a culture of trust can the corporation hope to achieve tangible business results from knowledge communities.

Knowledge communities, purposefully created for strategic business purposes, have the potential to build brand and reputation, create new markets, develop customer loyalty, and yield enormous intellectual capital dividends to their sponsoring organizations. But because they are human interactions—not technology solutions—realizing their potential requires consistent attention to those old-fashioned values that we learned in kindergarten: trust, sharing, and fair play.

References

[1] Kleiner and Roth, "How to Make Experience Your Company's Best Teacher," *Harvard Business Review* (September/October 1997).

[2] http://sws.caucus.com.

[3] www.egroups.com.

[4] David Weinbergier, "The Peer-to-Peer Future of Document Management," *Journal of the Hypedinked Organization* (December 18, 2000).

[5] Etienne Wenger, *Communities of Practice: Learning, Meaning, and Identity* (New York: Cambridge University Press, 1998).

[6]   Etienne Wenger, "Communities of Practice: Learning as a Social System" on-line at http://www.co-i-l.com/coil/knowledge-garden/cop/lss.shtml. First published in the *Systems Thinker* (June 1998).

[7]   Chris Collison, "Connecting the New Organization: How BP Amoco Encourages Postmerger Collaboration," *Knowledge Management Review* 7 (March/April 1999). www.km-review.com.

[8]   www.worldbank.org.

[9]   www.commerceone.com.

[10] www.commerceone.com/company/company.vision.html.

[11] www.trade-ranger.com.

[12] *Detroit Free Press*, www.freep.com.

Appendix A

Case studies list

Chapter 2

American Electric Power—Consolidated accounts payable activities to a single processing location

Essex and Suffolk Water—Customer relations management

Banco Hipotecarios—30 million paper loan documents converted into electronic images

Railroad Retirement Board—Retirement-survivor and unemployment-sickness benefits

Chapter 4

Fairfield University—Quantitative surveys

GTE Wireless—Quality of service

Retail Industry—Quick response system

Chapter 7

Eli Lilly—On-line learning and information sharing

Chapter 9

ON Semiconductor—User of on-line 100 directories

Chapter 10

BG Group—Knowledge sharing across the corporation

Chapter 11

@brint.com—Knowledge portal and global link

Telephone Industry—Home telephony competitive analysis

World Bank—Communities of practice across countries

Chapter 12

AT&T WorldNet—On-line forum for customer help

Commerce One—Building global Web-enabled marketplaces

Edmunds—Automotive pricing on-line

Appendix B

Selected bibliography

Allee, V. *The Knowledge Evolution*. Newton, MA: Butterworth-Heinemann, 1997.

Beniger, J. R. *The Control Revolution*. Cambridge, MA: Harvard University Press, 1986.

Bennis, W., and P. W. Biederman. *Organizing Genius: The Secrets of Creative Collaboration*. New York: Addison-Wesley, 1997.

Boisot, M. H. *Knowledge Assets*. New York: Oxford University Press, 1998.

Borgmann, A. *Holding on to Reality*. Chicago: The University of Chicago Press, 1999.

Branscom, A. *Who Owns Information?* New York: Basic Books, 1994.

Cutcher-Gershenfeld, J. *Knowledge-Driven Work*. New York: Oxford University Press, 1998.

Davenport, T., and L. Prusak. *Working Knowledge: How Organizations Manage What They Know*. Boston: Harvard Business School Press, 1998.

Devlin, K. *Infosense: Turning Information into Knowledge*. New York: W. H. Freeman, 1999.

Dizard, W. *The Coming Information Age*. White Plains, NY: Longman, 1989.

217

Eliot, T. S. *The Rock*. New York: Harcourt, Brace & Company, 1934.

Evans, P., and T. S. Wurster. *Blown to Bits: How the New Economics of Information Transforms Strategy*. Boston: Harvard Business School Press, 2000.

Gates, W. *The Road Ahead*. New York: Penguin Books, 1996.

Gates, W. *Business @ the Speed of Thought: Using a Digital Nervous System*. New York: Warner Books, 1999.

Glastonbury, B., and W. LaMendola. *The Integrity of Intelligence*. New York: St. Martin, 1992.

Hartman, A., J. Sifonis, and J. Kador. *Net Strategies for Success in the E-Conomy*. New York: McGraw-Hill, 2000.

Harvard Business School. *Harvard Business Review on Knowledge Management*. Boston: Harvard Business School Press, 1998.

Institute for Information Studies. *The Knowledge Economy: The Nature of Information in the Twenty-First Century*. Washington, DC: Institute for Information Studies, 1993.

Johnston, J. *Information Multiplicity: American Fiction in the Age of Media Saturation*. Baltimore: John Hopkins University Press, 1998.

McKibben, B. *The Age of Missing Information*. New York: Random House, 1992.

Morton, M. *The Corporation of the 1990s*. New York: Oxford University Press, 1991.

Neef, D. *The Knowledge Economy*. Boston: Butterworth-Heinemann, 1998.

O'Dell, C., C. J. Grayson, Jr., and N. Essaides. *If Only We Knew What We Know: The Transfer of Internal Knowledge and Best Practice*. New York: Free Press, 1998.

Peters, T. *Reinventing Work, the Project 50: Fifty Ways to Transform Every Task*. New York: Alfred A. Knopf, 1999.

Pfeffer, J., and R. I. Sutton. *The Knowing-Doing Gap*. Boston: Harvard Business School Press, 1999.

Prusak, L. *Knowledge in Organizations*. Boston: Butterworth-Heinemann, 1997.

Prusak, L., and T. H. Davenport. *Working Knowledge: How Organizations Manage What They Know.* Boston: Harvard Business School Press, 1998.

Reinertsen, D. G. *Managing the Design Factory: A Product Developer's Toolkit.* New York: Free Press, 1997.

Roos, J., G. Roos, L. Edvinsson, and N. Dragoneti. *Intellectual Capital.* New York: New York University Press, 1998.

Ruggles, R., and D. Holtshouse. *The Knowledge Advantage.* Dover, NH: Ernst & Young LLP, 1999.

Ruggles, R. "The State of the Notion: Knowledge Management in Practice." *The California Management Review* 40 (Spring 1998): 80.

Sakaiya, T. *The Knowledge Value Revolution or a History of the Future.* Tokyo: Kodansha International, 1985.

Shapiro, C., and H. R. Varian. *Information Rules: A Strategic Guide to the Network Economy.* Boston: Harvard Business School Press, 1999.

Appendix C

Glossary

Algorithm—A set of processes in a computer program used to solve a problem with a given set of steps.

Asynchronous Transfer Mode (ATM)—High-bandwidth, packet-like, multiplexing technique.

CDIA—Certified Document Imaging Architect.

CERN—Laboratory for particle physics in Geneva, Switzerland, and development center for HTML.

CKO—Chief Knowledge Officer.

Common Object Request Broker (CORBA)—The mechanism that enables objects to receive/ transmit requests with other objects.

Computer system architecture—Logical structure and relationship of the date and application functions used to satisfy business requirements.

Core data—Data, in their smallest form, needed to run the business.

Data mart—An easy-to-access data repository.

Data mining—Searching a database and making logical decisions based upon what is found.

Delphi—A forecasting method where several knowledgeable individuals make forecasts and a forecast is derived by a trained analyst from a weighted average.

Digital—A mode of transmission where information is coded in binary form for transmission on the network.

DIM—Document Imaging and Management Systems.

Directory services—Software that keeps track of users, their rights, and capabilities.

Domain name—Scheme in which host computers are specified.

E-mail—A service that allows text-form messages and attached files to be stored in a central file and retrieved with a modem-equipped terminal.

Enterprise—A large company organization generally concerning the whole corporation.

Epistemology—The theory of knowledge.

Feasibility analysis—A procedure for evaluating the technical and economic effectiveness of various alternatives.

Filter—A process or device that screens incoming information for definite characteristics and allows a subset of that information to pass through.

Firewall—Security software on servers and networks.

FTP—File transfer protocol.

Gateway—A system used to interconnect networks by converting the protocols of each network to those used by the other.

Groupware—Software used to share project, work effort, or product information.

Hypertext Markup Language (HTML)—Specifies encoding of information within Web pages.

Hypertext Transport Protocol (HTTP)—Specifies which Web pages are transported from the remote site to the browser.

Inference engine—The relationship generation (problem-solving part) of an expert system.

Information networking—The movement and use of information.

Interface—The connection between two systems.

Internet Service Provider (ISP)—Commercial organization providing Internet access.

KRAs—Key results areas, sometimes called critical success factors, are those things that must go right for an organization to succeed.

LAN—A local area network is a medium-to-high-speed data communications network restricted to a room, floor, or building. LANs that run between neighboring buildings are often called campus networks.

Legacy systems—Older systems (usually mainframe oriented) still performing enterprise functions.

Message transport agent—Software required to send e-mail between servers.

Metatag—Means of identifying data about data.

Modeling—A system for designing a network derived from a series of mathematical formulas that describe the behavior of various network elements.

MSA—Metropolitan Statistical Area.

Multipoint Internet Mail Extension (MIME)—Encodes nontext information within or attachment.

Outsourcing—Contracting out some or all of an organization's communications operations with the hope of leading to cost savings. The term is often used to cover any corporate activity that is contracted out.

Persistent Uniform Resource Locator (PURL)—Remembers links to old URLs.

Post Office Protocol (POP)—Performs client authentication and transfer of messages.

Private Branch Exchange (PBX)—A small version of the telephone company switching system usually located on a company's premises.

RFI—A request for information is issued by prospective purchasers to determine if a product or service is available and what its major features are.

RFP—A request for proposals is for specific proposals on a product or service where there are significant differences among products.

RFQ—A request for quotation is for price quotations about a product or service for which there is little difference in quality or features among competitors.

Router—Electronic transmission device that routes data packets to destinations.

Servers—They are devices in distributed computing networks that provide specialized services such as file, print, and modem or fax pool services.

Spam—Bulk e-mail usually sent by marketers.

Thin client—A workstation with limited functionality used for message switching.

Transmission Control Protocol/Internet Protocol (TCP/IP)—Standards to link computers across networks.

Triangulation—Gathering information from more than one source to help assure authenticity.

Uniform Resource Locator (URL)—Mechanism for identifying resources on the Internet.

Virtual circuit—A circuit established between two communicating devices by assigning a logical path over which data can flow. A virtual circuit can be either permanent, in which terminals are assigned a permanent path, or switched, in which the circuit is reestablished each time a terminal has data to send.

Virtual network—Can be a switched voice or data network offered by interexchange carriers that provides service similar to a private voice network. Virtual networks offer reduced rates.

Voice mail—A service that allows voice messages to be stored digitally in secondary storage and retrieved remotely by dialing access and identification codes.

Voice messaging—The use of digital technology on voice networks to record and play back messages.

VSAT—Very small aperture terminal is a small-diameter (typically 1.8 m to 2.4 m) satellite earth station situated at the customer's site and used for data, video, and occasionally voice communications.

WAN—Wide area networks consisting of leased and private circuits for voice and data service and generally operated by private, governmental, and institutional organizations.

X.400 Simple Mail Transfer Protocol—Standard for e-mail.

Contributors

About the editors

Richard F. Bellaver has 37 years of experience in telecommunications and data processing. He has developed software, supervised analyst and programmer teams, evaluated development software, and been a planner at the local and corporate level. He has been at Ball State University for 12 years, where he is the associate director of the Center for Information and Communications Sciences (CICS). He teaches courses in the history of the information and communications industry, human factors in design, telecommunications management, and strategic planning for information systems. He has consulted with a large telecommunications company regarding its entry into new business areas, has developed and led several product and system usability studies in conjunction with U.S. corporations, and was a director of the International Symposium on Telecommunications History. He was the originator and editor of the *CICS Journal*. Prior to Ball State, he was at AT&T headquarters, where he was the acting director for system engineering. He was responsible for the integration of the activities of the general departments, long lines, and information systems programming staffs. He was responsible for planning the analysis of all systems leading to the establishment of the computer systems architecture, the logical relationship of all applications and data. He helped establish the Data Stewardship Program at AT&T and helped supervise the integration of the activities of 13,000 programmers. At various times he held positions at Michigan Bell Company and Bell Telephone Laboratories. He is a graduate of Purdue University with a B.S.

in industrial economics. He attended Rutgers and Wayne State Universities, taking graduate economics courses, and has an M.B.A. from Michigan State. His e-mail address is rbellave@gw.bsu.edu.

John M. Lusa is a visiting associate professor for the Center for Information and Communication Sciences, a graduate school at Ball State University, where he teaches marketing and telecommunications management. He is also the principal for International Communications, his consulting firm in Centerville, Ohio. Mr. Lusa also writes about telecommunications and networking for a number of publications and has been project editor for several major magazine supplements. He has edited three editions of Auerbach's *The Network Manager's Handbook*, a 600-page reference manual. He is now the editor of Auerbach's *Data Communication Management* series. He retired as a publisher and editor-in-chief at PennWell Publishing Co. (Westford, Massachusetts), where he headed a number of publications in the networking and communications fields. Prior to that, he was a vice president, publisher, and editor-in-chief of a publication for information system executives, published by Hitchcock Publishing (Wheaton, Illinois), an ABC Publishing subsidiary at the time. He has also been in charge of computer advertising for the NCR Corp. in Dayton, Ohio, and later joined a large Chicago advertising agency, where he was the account supervisor for two computer firms. He is a journalism graduate of Ohio University and has an M.B.A. from the University of Dayton. He is active in the Association for Telecommunication Professionals in Columbus, Ohio, serves on the national alumni board of Ohio University, and is a retired colonel of the U.S. Army Reserves. He is also active in the Association of the U.S. Army. His e-mail address is Jmlusa@earthlink.net.

About the authors

Donald S. Byers is the director of the line of business for document management/imaging/workflow for Crowe, Chizek, and Co. and has been in the systems arena since 1970. His career started with IBM and Olivetti in the early 1970s. He cofounded Computer Systems of Indiana (CSI) in 1975. This company grew into one of the largest word processing distributors in the country. Later CSI (a multimillion dollar company) moved from dedicated word processing into software development and total solutions with applications developed in UNIX for reengineering county courts. Mr. Byers sold his company in 1988 and founded Imaging

Solutions of Indiana (ISI). This company was one of the first to implement imaging solutions for the GTE/Vantage program. ISI was merged into Crowe, Chizek and Co. in 1991 to start the document management/ imaging line of business. He has an A.S. degree in computer science and is a Fellow at Ball State University's CICS program.

Philip D. Campbell is an assistant professor at the J. Warren McClure School of Communication Systems Management of Ohio University, Athens, Ohio, where he teaches courses in the application and management of voice technologies, including call centers and computer telephony. Before joining the McClure School in 1996, he spent 14 years in software development, most recently at Cintech Tele-Management Systems, where he managed the development of automatic call distribution and call accounting systems. Previously, he held a series of positions at Telco Research Corporation, moving from analyst to manager in groups that developed software for voice network design and for call cost allocation and accounting. Campbell holds a B.S. in astronomy from the University of Michigan and M.S. degrees in physics from Louisiana State University and astronomy from the State University of New York at Stony Brook.

B. J. Deering is director of modeling and statistical analysis at Qwest Communications. She is responsible for providing data-based guidance for business decisions by developing new, predictive knowledge from diverse internal and external sources, including geographic and competitive intelligence systems. Previously, Dr. Deering managed primary and secondary market research functions, database marketing, and forecasting for major organizations, including US WEST, the Weyerhaeuser Company, BBDO Advertising, and the American Dairy Association. She has also managed corporate-wide systems for ongoing monitoring of views among employees, stakeholders, the public, and current and potential customers. Dr. Deering has a Ph.D. in consumer psychology from Purdue University, an M.S. in industrial-organizational psychology from the same university, and a B.S. in psychology from Duke University.

Elia Diamadatou is a Microsoft certified systems engineer (MCSE) for Superior Consultant, a company dedicated to the digital transformation of healthcare. She was born and raised in Athens, Greece, and moved to the United States in 1991. She attended Ball State University for both undergraduate and graduate studies and was the first international student to be awarded the Ball State presidential scholarship. She completed her B.S. in biology and immediately entered the graduate school at Ball State and earned an M.A. in biology, with an emphasis in the field of molecular genetics. She later entered the CICS, earning an additional masters degree in information and communications science.

Jay Edwin Gillette is a professor of information and communication sciences at Ball State University's CICS. Dr. Gillette teaches and conducts research in human communication; information networking design and development; telecommunications regulation, public policy, and economics; leadership and management for the Information Renaissance; and information theory. Previously, he was professor and associate chair of the Department of Information Networking and Telecommunications at Fort Hays State University in Kansas. He served as a Senior Policy Fellow at the Docking Institute of Public Affairs in Kansas and as a Senior Fellow of Information Technology and Telecommunications at the Center for the New West in Colorado, sponsored by US WEST and others. He worked at Bellcore (Bell Communications Research) in New Jersey, now named Telcordia Technologies. Previously, he was a professor at the Colorado School of Mines. He earned his Ph.D. and M.A. in English at the University of California, Berkeley, and his B.A. in literature at the University of California, San Diego.

Caitlin M. Groom is currently a manager with Deloitte Consulting, working in the Electronic Technology Infrastructure Group. She has been responsible for the design and implementation of IT solutions for trading exchanges and financial service companies, as well as manufacturing, entertainment, and healthcare organizations. She is a coauthor of the book *The Future of ATM and Broadband Networking* and a number of technical papers on networking and security.

Frank M. Groom is a professor in the graduate CICS at Ball State University. His research is concentrated in the areas of high-bandwidth networking, carrier backbone networks, metropolitan networks, distributed systems, and the storage of multimedia objects. Dr. Groom is the author of four books on high-bandwidth networking, including *The ATM Handbook* from IEEE Press, as well as *The Future of IP and Packet Networking*, *The Future of ATM and Broadband Networking*, and *Multimedia over the Broadband Network* from the International Engineering Press. He is currently working on a new book—*Strategies for CLECs*. He has over 100 books published. He has taught courses at IBM, Digital Equipment Corporation, AT&T, McDonalds, Ford, Anixter, and for Motorola in Hong Kong and Macao. He has presented lectures at Beijing University of Posts and Telecommunications in China, Ecole National Superiore des Telecommunications de Bretagne in France, and Bielefeld University in Germany. He received his Ph.D. in information systems from the University of Wisconsin and is the former senior director of information systems for Ameritech.

Steve Jones is currently an associate professor at the CICS at Ball State University. Prior to coming to higher education, he was owner and applications engineer for one of the country's largest interconnect companies, providing telecommunications solutions to commercial clients. He has implemented wide area voice and data networks as well as designed distance learning communities for higher-education applications. He holds undergraduate degrees in psychology and engineering technology. His masters and doctoral studies were done with cognate areas of technology education. His current research interests include wireless local loop technologies, competitive local exchange carriers, and qualitative research applied to technical environments.

Ronald J. Kovac is an associate professor at the CICS, Ball State University. He has a long-term relationship with the CICS. During the early years of the CICS program, Dr. Kovac was a member of the College of Practical and Applied Arts and taught courses in the Industry and Technology Department. During the first 2 years of the Center, Dr. Kovac volunteered to instruct a CICS course. He left the university and became the telecommunications manager for the State University of New York (SUNY). In this role, Dr. Kovac designed and implemented the wide area network connecting 64 university sites in the state of New York. Dr. Kovac also led the migration of the network into frame relay and spearheaded the integration of legacy systems into TCP/IP. He subsequently returned to Ball State University, joining the CICS faculty. Dr. Kovac received an A.A.S. from SUNY in 1974 with a major in electrical technology and a concentration in computers. He received a B.S. from SUNY in 1977 and an M.S. in 1981. His major area of focus was industrial education. He received his Ph.D. from Indiana State University in 1985.

Larry L. Learn is the former director of telecommunications planning for OCLC, Inc., Dublin, Ohio. He holds a B.A. (1965) in physics and mathematics and an M.A. (1967) in nuclear physics from Western Michigan University and is a graduate of the Central States Universities–Argonne National Laboratory Honors Program in Physics conducted under the auspices of the University of Chicago. He completed work toward his Ph.D in nuclear instrumentation at Michigan State University and is a graduate of the Executive Education Program of the Harvard

Graduate School of Business. He has published numerous articles and contributed to several books in the fields of nuclear physics and accelerator design, computer and information science, and telecommunications. He is the author of *Telecommunications for Information Specialists*. He is a founder and director emeritus of The Association of Telecommunications Professionals, Columbus, Ohio, and has taught at Western Michigan University and Michigan State University. He is now consulting. His e-mail address is learnl@netzero.net.

Josh Plaskoff is a member of the Corporate Knowledge Management (KM) Group at Eli Lilly and Co. and has been leading the development of the corporate KM strategy. He has been designing knowledge-based solutions for over 13 years. He holds a degree in English and a master's degree in educational psychology and technology. While at Xerox Corporation, Mr. Plaskoff led both traditional training and knowledge technology solutions, after which he consulted for a number of Fortune 500 companies in the development of knowledge systems. He is currently pursuing his Ph.D. at Indiana University in instructional systems technology, specializing in KM. His e-mail address is jplaskoff@lilly.com.

Ken Pratt joined British Gas (now BG plc) some 20 years ago, after completing his doctorate in theoretical chemistry. His career has largely been involved with the development and deployment of advanced information technology systems for the company, first as a developer and then as a manager. These systems include gas supply scheduling, gas transmission network optimization, condensate reservoir simulation, and chemical plant design. For the past few years, he has also managed BG technology projects on emerging technologies in information technology. In 1997 he was appointed as project manager for the company's strategic project on technology knowledge management. This has the aim of enabling ready access to gas chain technology information for all BG employees around the world. He now leads a significant portfolio of projects in the KM arena

Michael L. Simpson was fomerly Chief Marketing Officer for Interact Commerce Corporation (previously known as SalesLogix), Scottsdale, Arizona. He was formerly Director of Strategic Market Planning for Novell, Inc., and has been in the software industry since 1987. In this capacity he was a major contributor to Novell's corporate strategy and is responsible for strategic market planning in many key business sectors associated with emerging markets. He is a respected industry expert on directory services and Novell's Internet products. He has appeared in the global business and industry press, including *US News & World Report, The Washington Post*, CNN, and CNBC. Further, he has provided extensive industry expertise at conferences worldwide, having spoken in more than 15 countries about the industry's future and Novell's strategic vision. Prior to joining Novell, Simpson was general manager of a large network integration and consulting firm. He now operates 5th Line, Inc. (Phoenix, Arizona). His e-mail address is michael@5thline.com.

Barbara Weaver Smith is the president of Smith Weaver Smith, Inc. (SWS), a leadership and project management firm focused on accelerated cultural transformations in business and communities. Dr. Weaver works with executives and entrepreneurs in change environments to manage joint ventures, collaborative projects, mergers, and rapid growth. Her clients include financial services companies, technology firms, schools, universities, and community foundations. On-line communications and strategic planning events help to accelerate cultural change. Prior to managing SWS, she was president and CEO of the Indiana Humanities Council (1994–1998), a nonprofit organization whose mission is to influence positive cultural change through public engagement with history, philosophy, literature, and philanthropy. There she honed her skills in strategic planning, marketing, and relationship management while coordinating local and statewide programs on civics, philanthropy, international awareness, and living history. At Ball State University (1985–1994), Dr. Weaver held dual appointments as professor of English and Dean of the University College, an undergraduate college providing academic support services to freshmen, nontraditional students, and student athletes. Her academic career began at Anderson University (1973–1985), where she was an associate professor of English and directed the Learning Center and the Writing Program. She earned a B.A. in English and history from Anderson University and an M.A. and a Ph.D. in English from Ball State University. She completed the Institute for Educational Management at Harvard University in 1991 and is an active writer who publishes the e-newsletter and on-line journal "Talking Culture, Talking Knowledge." She hosts and facilitates more than a dozen on-line discussions at the Smith Weaver Smith Learning Community, http://sws.caucus.com. Her e-mail address is bsmith@smith-weaversmith.com.

Feng Kwei Wang is an assistant professor in the School of Information Science and Learning Technologies at the University of Missouri,

Columbia, Missouri. He has three advanced degrees in computer science, business administration, and educational technology. Over the past 10 years, he has been development consultant for several Fortune 500 companies including AT&T, IBM, Delco Electronics, and Eli Lilly. He is interested in the process of designing and developing information systems, the uses of multimedia technologies to enhance human performance, and the design and implementation of KM systems. His e-mail address is wangfeng@missouri.edu.

Index

Multimedia Database Management Systems, Guojun Lu

Practical Guide to Software Quality Management, John W. Horch

Practical Process Simulation Using Object-Oriented Techniques and C++, José Garrido

Secure Messaging with PGP and S/MIME, Rolf Oppliger

Security Fundamentals for E-Commerce, Vesna Hassler

Security Technologies for the World Wide Web, Rolf Oppliger

Software Fault Tolerance Techniques and Implementation, Laura L. Pullum

Software Verification and Validation for Practitioners and Managers, Second Edition, Steven R. Rakitin

Strategic Software Production with Domain-Oriented Reuse, Paolo Predonzani, Giancarlo Succi, and Tullio Vernazza

Systems Modeling for Business Process Improvement, David Bustard, Peter Kawalek, and Mark Norris, editors

User-Centered Information Design for Improved Software Usability, Pradeep Henry

Workflow Modeling: Tools for Process Improvement and Application Development, Alec Sharp and Patrick McDermott

For further information on these and other Artech House titles, including previously considered out-of-print books now available through our In-Print-Forever® (IPF®) program, contact:

Artech House
685 Canton Street
Norwood, MA 02062
Phone: 781-769-9750
Fax: 781-769-6334
e-mail: artech@artechhouse.com

Artech House
46 Gillingham Street
London SW1V 1AH UK
Phone: +44 (0)20 7596-8750
Fax: +44 (0)20 7630-0166
e-mail: artech-uk@artechhouse.com

Find us on the World Wide Web at:
www.artechhouse.com